A WORLD BANK COUNTRY STUDY

Bangladesh

*From Counting the Poor
to Making the Poor Count*

*The World Bank
Washington, D.C.*

D1399680

CONTENTS

FIGURES

TABLES

ANNEX TABLES

ABSTRACT

Reducing poverty is the central development challenge in Bangladesh. Who are the poor? Where do they live? What are the characteristics of poor households? Has poverty declined over time? Has inequality increased? In answering these "*counting the poor*" questions, this country study provides a poverty profile for Bangladesh. As importantly, the study addresses several questions about "*making the poor count*" in the choice, design, and implementation of public policies and programs that aim to reduce poverty. What is the relationship between growth and inequality? Is this relationship different for rural and urban areas? Does education reduce poverty? How much do the poor benefit from increasing public spending on health and education? Are households that own more land less poor? Do area characteristics such as rural infrastructure affect the incidence of poverty? How cost-effective are safety net programs? Where do micro-finance programs fit within a poverty reduction strategy? Do they reach the poorest? How well do NGO services in education and health compete with public and private services? This report is also part of a process of strengthening capacity and enhancing poverty data and analysis in Bangladesh. In late 1994 World Bank staff undertook a collaborative, capacity-building initiative with the Bangladesh Bureau of Statistics (BBS) to help enhance the 1995-96 Household Expenditure Survey (HES), train BBS staff, improve basic data analysis, and publish an abstract. This work is still continuing through capacity-building assistance for the Household Expenditure Survey for 1999-2000.

ACKNOWLEDGMENTS

This study was prepared by a World Bank team consisting of Syed Nizamuddin, Martin Ravallion, Shekhar Shah (team leader), and Quentin Wodon. Michael Walton and Peter Lanjouw were the internal peer reviewers. Zahid Hussain, Juan Munoz, Bala Bhaskar Naidu, and Salman Zaidi provided valuable inputs. Jillian Badami provided administrative support. Afsana Ahmad provided research assistance. The report was edited by Ilyse Zable and processed by Jillian Badami with assistance from Lin Chin.

This report is one of the outcomes of an ongoing capacity building effort by the World Bank to strengthen the capabilities of the Bangladesh Bureau of Statistics for poverty data collection and analysis. The assistance of Mr. Waliul Islam, Secretary Statistics, Mr. Abdul Jabbar, Project Director, and other Bureau staff is gratefully acknowledged. The background work for this report was discussed at a seminar jointly sponsored by the Government of Bangladesh and the World Bank in Dhaka in May 1997 and in subsequent discussions in Dhaka in August 1997 and February 1998. Comments from the participants at these discussions are gratefully acknowledged. This report was originally released in April 1998.

ACRONYMS AND ABBREVIATIONS

ADAB	-	Association of Development Agencies in Bangladesh
ADP	-	Annual Development Program
ASA	-	Association for Social Advancement
BBS	-	Bangladesh Bureau of Statistics
BIDS	-	Bangladesh Institute of Development Studies
BRDB	-	Bangladesh Rural Development Board
CBN	-	Cost of basic needs
CIRDAP	-	Center for Integrated Rural Development for Asia and the Pacific
DCI	-	Direct caloric intake
FEI	-	Food energy intake
FFE	-	Food for Education
FFW	-	Food for Work
GDP	-	Gross domestic product
GNP	-	Gross national product
HES	-	Household Expenditure Survey
HPSS	-	Health and Population Sector Strategy
IFPRI	-	International Food Policy Research Institute
LFS	-	Labor Force Survey
LGED	-	Local Government Engineering Department
LSMS	-	Living Standards Measurement Survey
NGO	-	Nongovernmental organization
PKSF	-	Palli Karma Sahayak Foundation
SSC	-	Secondary school certificate
TR	-	Test Relief
VGD	-	Vulnerable Group Development

CURRENCY EQUIVALENT
Taka (Tk)
US$1.00 = Tk 46.30 (April 28, 1998)

GOVERNMENT'S FISCAL YEAR
July 1- June 30

EXECUTIVE SUMMARY

COUNTING THE POOR AND MAKING THE POOR COUNT

1.   Reducing poverty is the central development challenge in Bangladesh. This poverty assessment answers several basic questions about counting the poor. Who are the poor? How numerous are they? Where do they live? What are the characteristics of poor households? Has poverty declined? Has inequality increased? In answering these questions this poverty assessment constructs a poverty profile for Bangladesh.

2.   As importantly, the poverty assessment addresses several questions about how to make the poor count in the choice, design, and implementation of public policies and programs whose aim is to reduce poverty. These questions are more difficult: What is the relationship between growth and inequality? Is this relationship different for rural and urban areas? Does education reduce poverty? How much do the poor benefit from increasing public spending on health and education? Are households that own more land less poor? Do area characteristics such as rural infrastructure affect the incidence of poverty? How cost-effective are safety net programs? Where do microfinance programs fit within a poverty reduction strategy? Do they reach the poorest? How well do NGO services in education and health compete with public and private services?

3.   The lack of access to primary data on poverty in Bangladesh has been a serious, long-standing hurdle to more detailed poverty analysis. Official poverty estimates have been shrouded in some controversy because independent analysts have never been able to fully replicate the estimates, examine the strengths and weaknesses of the official methodology, or suggest alternative estimates using primary data. Recognizing these problems, in late 1994 World Bank staff undertook a collaborative, capacity-building initiative with the Bangladesh Bureau of Statistics (BBS) to help enhance the 1995-96 Household Expenditure Survey (HES), train BBS staff, improve basic data analysis, and publish an abstract. This initiative has also led to a series of analytical papers using the 1995-96 and earlier HES data (these are listed in the Bibliography). This report is part of this process. Work is still underway to mainstream poverty analysis into public policy design, implementation, and evaluation.

IMPORTANT FINDINGS AND POLICY CONCLUSIONS

4.   *Poverty measurement has been put on a sounder footing.* The BBS has now adopted the cost of basic needs method for estimating poverty incidence, which is preferable to the official methodology used in the past. Using primary data from successive rounds of the HES between 1983 and 1996, chapter 1 estimates the incidence of poverty over time calculated according to the cost of basic needs method. Two sets of poverty lines identify the very poor (lower poverty line) and the poor (upper poverty line).

5.   *Poverty has declined in the 1990s, but the remaining challenges are massive.* Both the lower and the upper poverty lines indicate a statistically significant decline in poverty after 1991-92. The incidence of the very poor declined from 43 percent of the population in 1991-92 to 36 percent in 1995-96; the incidence of the poor declined from 59 to 53 percent. Although poverty has declined in both rural and urban areas, rural poverty is still higher than urban poverty. Reducing the poverty of the very poor living in rural areas—still at 40 percent of the rural population in 1995-96—remains a massive challenge.

6.   ***Rising inequality has reduced the rate of poverty reduction.*** The decline in poverty observed in the 1990s contrasts with the stagnation of poverty in the 1980s. Why was overall poverty reduction so slow or nonexistent over the 1980s? This complex question requires considerable inquiry, particularly since average GDP growth was roughly around 4 percent and exceeded the declining population growth rate. Chapter 2 shows that part of the explanation is rising inequality. Depending on which poverty measure is used, one-fifth to one-third of the potential poverty reduction from growth may have been lost because of higher inequality. The higher inequality associated with growth in Bangladesh does not imply that growth should not be pursued. To the contrary, faster growth is needed if poverty is to be reduced faster, because the net effect of growth on poverty reduction is positive. But in addition to faster growth, efforts to limit rising inequality are required. Over the period 1991-92 to 1995-96, inequality rose the least with agricultural growth, and as a result the net elasticity of poverty with respect to growth was the largest in agriculture. Assuming these elasticities hold unchanged in the future, growth in agriculture would tend to reduce poverty and limit inequality more than identical growth in industry and services. Industry and services, however, are likely to grow much faster than agriculture, as they have done in the past, and the net contribution of faster industrial and service growth to poverty reduction should be quite high.

7.   ***The gains from education and other household and regional characteristics suggest areas for policy emphasis.*** Apart from broad-based growth, targeted investments in the poor's human and physical capital can reduce poverty and limit inequality. Which investments should have priority? This is a difficult question, but chapter 3 provides some partial answers. Education and land ownership remain key determinants of living standards. The gains from education are high and have persisted over time. Higher education has the largest impact in urban areas. Land ownership matters more in rural areas. The returns to education, as measured by a household's per capita consumption, are similar for the household head and spouse. Differences in poverty between geographical areas depend more on differences in area characteristics than on differences in the characteristics of the households living in those areas. This finding suggests that investment policies aimed at poor areas will reduce poverty. Occupation, too, affects living standards. In rural areas, for example, the gains from switching from the farm to the nonfarm sector are positive and large for the poor, implying that developing the rural nonfarm sector holds considerable potential for poverty reduction.

8.   ***Public expenditures reduce poverty, but their targeting and efficiency must be improved.*** The share of expenditures in the Annual Development Program devoted to social sector spending has more than doubled since the early 1990s and is expected to increase further in the years ahead, especially the share devoted to education and health. Chapter 4 reviews the performance of public services in these two areas. The case for substantial public expenditures to education and health is strong on externality and equity grounds. While public expenditures on health appear to be somewhat better targeted to the poor than public expenditure on education, there is much scope for improvement in increasing the quality of and access to such services. Government programs, such as Food for Work, Vulnerable Group Development, Test Relief, and Rural Maintenance are well targeted. A detailed assessment of Food for Education, the fastest growing program, shows that it raises primary school attendance and is cost-effective as measured by its long-term impact. But, it is not as well-targeted as the other programs, and improvements in targeting and internal efficiency would further raise its social returns. Investments in the program's growth will have to be balanced with the need to improve the overall quality of primary education.

9.   ***Bangladesh's NGOs are a unique, vital resource for faster poverty reduction, and more needs to be done to support partnerships with them.*** Bangladesh is a world leader in innovative NGO programs. Chapter 5 reviews the growth of NGOs and their performance in delivering microcredit,

particularly to the very poor. With rapid growth in microcredit, it will be important to ensure that quantitative objectives (reaching as many households as possible) are not pursued at the cost of qualitative objectives (reaching the households that most need assistance). The government and microcredit providers should look for ways, possibly through innovative partnerships, to reach the poorest, as well as better-off borrowers who are ineligible for microcredit but do not have access to formal credit. A village-based survey provides new insights into the superiority of rural health and education services provided by NGOs rather than the government or the private sector. The vastly superior performance of NGO social services suggests clear possibilities for partnerships among NGOs, the government, and the private sector in providing better health and education services. This information also sheds light on the potential priority areas for improving government services: quality appears to be the major problem with public health facilities, and both quality and quantity appear to be problems in public education.

BUILDING CONSENSUS FOR A POVERTY REDUCTION STRATEGY

10.   This report is part of a long-term process of capacity building and mainstreaming of poverty analysis in Bangladesh.[1] Its findings outlined above suggest five pillars of a possible poverty reduction strategy—accelerating economic growth; promoting education for the poor, particularly primary education, and particularly for girls; investing in poor areas to take advantage of strong location effects on poverty reduction; improved targeting of public expenditures and safety nets to reach the poor better; and forming further partnerships with NGOs to reach the poorest and not-so-poor in ways designed to make a stronger attack on poverty.

11.   Discussions with stakeholders, NGOs, the government, poverty researchers, and other donors in Bangladesh arising from this report will help to build support for an action plan and more detailed policy and institutional changes for faster poverty reduction. In line with the capacity-building emphasis of the World Bank's country assistance strategy, these discussions will also help to build consensus on the institutional capacity required to mainstream poverty analysis in policy design and implementation. BBS will field the next Household Expenditure Survey in 1999. This will provide the opportunity and the means to further refine our understanding of the determinants of poverty and the conditions under which households in rural and urban Bangladesh can most easily escape poverty.

---

1 In addition to this report, two other tools have been developed to facilitate the use of the poverty assessment. First, the poverty assessment and its background papers are available on the World Bank's web site (http://www.worldbank.org/html/extdr/offrep/sas/bangladesh-poverty/). Second, an easy-to-use spreadsheet has been prepared to allow analysts and policymakers to simulate poverty measures based on chosen household characteristics and to explore the impact of policies that change these characteristics. This spreadsheet is also available at the web site.

OVERVIEW OF CHAPTER 1: BUILDING CAPACITY AND MEASURING POVERTY

PARA.	KEY CONCLUSIONS	POLICY IMPLICATIONS
1.5 to 1.8	**Improving data collection** The Household Expenditure Survey (HES) provides the basic national data for poverty analysis. Bank staff have assisted the Bangladesh Bureau of Statistics (BBS) in enhancing the data collection and entry procedures for the 1995-96 HES. Consequently, data became available and were analyzed much faster than in previous survey rounds. The HES is now an integrated survey that includes a rural community module and a special-topic, rotating module (education in 1995-96).	The BBS should continue to improve the HES in order to enhance its timeliness and use for policy analysis. For the next HES, a topic for the rotating module will need to be selected. The household questionnaire could include more questions on participation in social and NGO programs to provide data for program evaluation. Qualitative assessment techniques, particularly for health and education, could usefully complement the existing HES.
1.9 to 1.11	**Building analytical capability** Disagreements have persisted for many years about the extent of poverty and its trend, in large part because of methodological differences on poverty measurement. Bank staff have assisted and trained BBS personnel to use the cost of basic needs method. The BBS used this method for estimating poverty incidence in the *Summary Report on the Household Expenditure Survey 1995-96*. The BBS now provides access to HES data for bona fide research uses.	BBS staff should be further trained on economics of poverty and on the use of household data to inform public policy. This will lead to better questionnaire design and higher quality data. There is a need to mainstream poverty analysis in the design of public and NGO poverty programs. The government should set up a working group consisting of the BBS, researchers, donor agencies, and line ministries to pursue this.
1.12 to 1.19	**Trends in poverty** Thirty six percent of the population in 1995-96 was *very poor*, a significant drop from 43 percent in 1991-92 (when poverty was still higher than its 1983-84 level of 41 percent). Forty percent of the rural and 14 percent of the urban population was very poor. Nationally, 53 percent of the population was *poor*, 57 percent of the rural, and 35 percent of the urban population. Urban poverty has declined the most. Ninety three percent of the very poor and 89 percent of the poor live in rural areas.	Economic growth in which the poor can participate must accelerate if poverty is to decline faster. The needs of the rural poor and the poorest require special attention in government, NGO, and donor-funded programs.
1.20	**Trends in inequality** Inequality has increased, particularly since 1991-92. This contrasts with the experience of developing countries as a whole, but some other semirural economies such as China have had similar experiences. Inequality is higher in urban than in rural areas. The gap in rural-urban living standards has increased, indicating that rural areas are lagging behind. Rising inequality within the rural and urban sectors also accounts for a large share of rising inequality nationally.	Programs that reduce inequality without jeopardizing growth must be developed further. These include effective safety nets, improved access to better quality primary education and social services in health and family planning, and investments designed to raise the human and physical capital of poor people and poor regions.
1.21 to 1.32	**Poverty profile** There are large differences in poverty by region within the urban and rural sectors and by education, land ownership, occupation, and demographics. Female-headed households are poorer in rural areas, and women have less education and employment. Village attitudes towards women's activities suggest broad support among men and women for women's education, but less support among men than women for participation in income-generating activities.	Growth alone is not sufficient to reduce poverty. At the regional and household levels, public policies must target vulnerable groups. Attitudes toward women are an important social determinant of equity, access to services, and well-being. Widespread support for women's education suggests that more needs to be done to provide schooling for girls, and the strong support among women for income-generating activities suggests a larger role for microcredit or other support for nonfarm self- and wage employment.
1.33 to 1.35	**International comparisons** Although Bangladesh has reduced poverty and improved other dimensions of well-being, it lags behind other countries in South and East Asia. Indonesia, for example, had a GNP per capita similar to that of Bangladesh in the early 1970s, but (notwithstanding its recent problems) has reduced poverty and improved its social indicators much faster since then.	A combination of high growth, good social policies, and investment in human capital can help Bangladesh to achieve the rapid rates of poverty reduction of the East Asian countries. Bangladesh should learn from the pro-growth policies adopted in these countries to promote faster growth with equity.

CHAPTER 1: BUILDING CAPACITY AND MEASURING POVERTY

1.1   Reducing poverty is the central development challenge in Bangladesh. This poverty assessment addresses several basic "counting the poor" questions: Who are the poor? How numerous are they? Where do they live? What are the characteristics of poor households? How should we measure poverty? Has poverty declined? Has inequality increased? This study also discusses equally important questions about "making the poor count" in the choice, design, and implementation of public policies and programs aimed at reducing poverty. This discussion requires answers to more difficult questions: What is the relationship between growth and inequality? Is this relationship different for rural and urban areas? Is education associated with lower poverty rates? How much do the poor benefit from increasing public spending on health and education? Are households that own more land less poor? Do area characteristics such as rural infrastructure affect poverty? How effective are safety net programs that seek to protect the poor and the most vulnerable?

1.2   Bangladesh is blessed with world-renowned nongovernmental organizations (NGOs) and microfinance institutions such as BRAC and Grameen Bank. We examine several questions relating to NGO activities. Where does microfinance fit in an overall poverty reduction strategy? How well does it reach the poorest? How well do NGO services in education and health compete with public and private services? How should these services be divided among the public, NGO, and private sectors to maximize the impact on poverty?

1.3   The World Bank's most recent poverty assessment for Bangladesh was based on aggregate, secondary data and the published official estimates of poverty (World Bank 1990). Without access to primary data, it could not capture the important characteristics of the poor needed to construct a poverty profile and elucidate the determinants of poverty. The lack of public access to primary data has been a serious, long-standing hurdle to better poverty analysis in Bangladesh. Further, official poverty estimates have been controversial, because independent analysts, without access to data, have never been able to fully replicate the estimates or examine the pros and cons of official methodologies.

1.4   We are in a better position today, thanks to a long-term, collaborative, capacity-building effort between the Bangladesh Bureau of Statistics (BBS) and the World Bank. The next section outlines this collaboration. The third section presents new measures of national, rural, and urban poverty since 1983, based on the last five rounds of the Household Expenditure Survey (HES), the basic national data for poverty analysis. The fourth section discusses poverty measures based on location, land ownership, and the education, gender, and occupation of the household head. The final section compares Bangladesh's overall performance with that of other South and East Asian countries.

BUILDING CAPACITY FOR MEASURING AND ANALYZING POVERTY

1.5   As part of the joint capacity-building effort with the Bank, the BBS designed and fielded an improved HES in 1995-96. It also improved the official methodology for measuring poverty and granted researchers access to the HES data. Work on mainstreaming poverty analysis into public policy design, implementation, and evaluation is still underway; this poverty report is part of the process.

The Household Expenditure Survey is improved
1.6   The Bank's South Asia Region started its capacity-building effort with the BBS in 1994. The cooperative effort centered initially on the design for the 1995-96 HES. The Survey was made an integrated survey by adding to the basic household questionnaire a special-purpose module designed to

rotate among different topics and to collect detailed information for each household member on the chosen topic (BBS 1997e). The BBS chose education for the 1995-96 HES. It also integrated into the survey a rural community module to obtain detailed information on the villages (rural primary sampling units) from which households were selected.

1.7   *The survey methodology has been enhanced.* The BBS also introduced important innovations in its data collection and entry procedures along the lines of the World Bank's Living Standard Measurement Surveys (LSMS). The use of personal computers to enter and validate data in the field improved data quality, since households could be revisited soon after they were surveyed to correct logical errors or verify unusual entries (see BBS 1997f for details on the sampling framework, survey methodology, and field procedures). The previous practice of processing the HES questionnaires on mainframe computers in Dhaka long after the data had been collected would have made this impossible. That older method also forced long delays before poverty estimates could be published (for example, the preliminary report for the 1991-92 HES was published only in 1995, and the full report in 1997). In contrast, the preliminary 1995-96 HES data were available for analysis four months after the survey was completed, and the BBS published a summary report (BBS 1997e), including new poverty measures, considerably faster than it had in previous HES rounds.

1.8   *BBS staff were trained and a broader dialogue has been started on poverty issues.* The comparative advantage of BBS is in collecting timely, high-quality data, not in conducting research. Nonetheless, a good understanding of poverty measurement and analysis can greatly help to improve data collection. To this end, 12 BBS staff participated in a specially designed, two-week workshop on poverty analysis arranged by World Bank staff in May 1997 in Kathmandu (officials from the Nepal Central Bureau of Statistics also took part in the training). The hands-on workshop included sessions on data management, poverty analysis, and public policy. Each participant had exclusive access to a personal computer and used data from the Bangladesh HES and the Nepal LSMS. The workshop was followed by seminars organized jointly with the government in Dhaka to discuss the preliminary findings from the 1995-96 and earlier HES data and the background work for this report. These seminars and the ongoing collaboration with the BBS has promoted a dialogue among the government, researchers, and donors on how to best mainstream poverty analysis in public policy formulation, with the objective of making poverty analysis a much more integral part of designing and evaluating government and NGO policies and programs. The May 1998 meeting of Bangladesh's aid donors at the Bangladesh Development Forum in Dhaka will pay special attention to poverty issues.

BBS has adopted the superior cost of basic needs method for measuring poverty
1.9   A poverty measure needs three elements:
   - An indicator of well-being or welfare, such as per capita caloric intake or per capita real expenditures.
   - A normative threshold—a poverty line—representing the minimal well-being a person or household must attain to be above poverty.
   - An aggregate measure to assess poverty across the population. One example is the headcount ratio or index, which indicates the percentage of the population whose welfare indicator falls below the poverty line.

1.10   The three methods used for estimating poverty in Bangladesh differ in which indicator of welfare they use and how they define the poverty line (table 1.1 and Background Paper 5[1]). The direct calorie

[1] The background papers prepared for this poverty report are part of the World Bank's ongoing work on poverty in Bangladesh. They are listed in the Bibliography.

intake and food energy intake methods have been used in the past for official poverty estimates, while the cost of basic needs method has more often been used by independent researchers in Bangladesh and abroad. Ideally, poverty measures should be *representative* and *consistent*. They are representative if the indicator used for measuring welfare reflects people's lack of command over basic goods and services associated with poverty; they are consistent if they are based on poverty lines that represent the same living standard for different groups and over time. The direct calorie intake method is not representative, while the food energy intake method is not consistent (see the Annex for details). The cost of basic needs method is typically consistent and representative.

Table 1.1: Strengths and Weaknesses of Alternative Methods of Measuring Poverty

	Direct calorie intake	Food energy intake	Cost of basic needs
Welfare indicator	Caloric intake in kilocalories (kcal)	Consumption expenditures in taka	Consumption expenditures in taka
Poverty line	Caloric threshold (usually 2,122 kcal per person per day)	Expenditure level at which households are expected to reach the caloric threshold	Expenditure level at which households can afford predetermined basic consumption needs
Strengths and weaknesses	Comparisons over time consistent, but welfare indicator narrow and not representative of what individuals actually consume	Indicator representative of actual consumption, but poverty comparisons and poverty lines not consistent across time and space	Indicator representative and poverty comparisons consistent across time and space for real expenditures

1.11 *Calculating the cost of basic needs poverty lines.* In its *Summary Report of the Household Expenditure Survey 1995-96* (BBS 1997e), the BBS dropped the food energy intake method and has instead adopted the cost of basic needs method (it has retained the direct calorie intake method for comparisons with its previous estimates). The cost of basic needs method is based on the estimation of the cost of a bundle of goods that meets predetermined basic needs, which are held constant from year to year and across space and groups. Three steps are needed to estimate this cost, which then defines the poverty line (see the Annex and Background Papers 4 and 6 for details). *First*, a representative, fixed food bundle must be defined to meet the nutritional norm of 2,122 kcal a day per person. The cost of this food bundle is calculated for various geographic areas using estimates of the price of each food item (as paid by the poor) in each area. This cost represents the food poverty line for each area (Annex table A1.1). *Second*, allowances for nonfood consumption are estimated. These are also area-specific in order to capture geographic differences in the costs of nonfood goods. A fixed bundle for nonfood consumption is not used because of the intrinsic difficulty of defining a basic, representative nonfood bundle. Instead, lower (less generous) and upper (more generous) allowances for nonfood basic needs are computed for each area based on households' actual nonfood expenditures (Annex table A1.2).[2] *Third*, for each area the food poverty line is summed with the lower and upper allowances for nonfood consumption, to yield, respectively, the lower and upper poverty lines. The lower poverty lines can be said to identify the very poor, and the upper poverty lines the poor.

---

[2] The lower nonfood allowance is the nonfood expenditure of households whose *total* consumption expenditures are equal to the food poverty line (the very poor), meaning that anything they spend on nonfood actually reduces their food expenditures below the food poverty line. The upper nonfood allowance is computed from the nonfood expenditures of households whose *food* expenditures are equal to the food poverty line (the poor). See the Annex for details.

MEASURING THE INCIDENCE OF POVERTY

1.12   This section examines the trends in poverty incidence and inequality between 1983 and 1996. It is based on the lower and upper poverty lines estimated with the cost of basic needs method and the primary data from the HES of 1983-84, 1985-86, 1988-89, 1991-92, and 1995-96.

Poverty has decreased significantly in the 1990s

1.13   In 1995-96, 36 percent of Bangladesh's population was very poor and 53 percent was poor (figures 1.1a, 1.1b, table 1.2). The incidence of poverty has declined since 1991-92 as measured by both the lower and upper poverty lines. Assuming poverty incidence for 1985-86 was underestimated because the estimates are not consistent with other evidence and because the HES for that year was of lower quality,[3] poverty incidence was relatively stable from 1983-84 to 1991-92, and then experienced a statistically significant decrease in 1995-96. The drop in poverty in recent years was larger in urban than in rural areas. Throughout the period under review, rural poverty remained much higher than urban poverty as measured with both the lower and upper poverty lines.

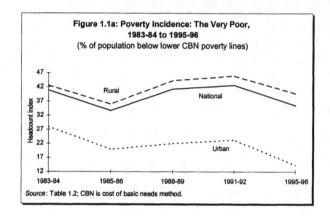

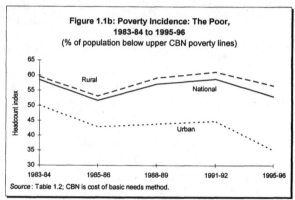

Table 1.2: Headcount Indices of Poverty with the Cost of Basic Needs Method, 1983-84 to 1995-96
(percentage of population below the poverty line)

	Very poor (lower poverty line)					Poor (upper poverty line)				
	1983-84	1985-86	1988-89	1991-92	1995-96	1983-84	1985-86	1988-89	1991-92	1995-96
National	40.91	33.77	41.32	42.69	35.55	58.50	51.73	57.13	58.84	53.08
Rural	42.62	36.01	44.30	45.95	39.76	59.61	53.14	59.18	61.19	56.65
Urban	28.03	19.90	21.99	23.29	14.32	50.15	42.92	43.88	44.87	35.04

Note: See Annex for the definition of the poverty lines. The figures for 1995-96 are also reported in BBS (1997e).
Source: World Bank staff estimates.

Independent evidence also suggests declining poverty in the 1990s

1.14   *Other estimates of poverty incidence.* The cost of basic needs headcount indices are broadly consistent with two sets of independent studies of poverty conducted in the late 1980s and early 1990s. The first set uses grouped aggregate data available in the various HES reports published by the BBS and

---

3 Concerns have been raised about the validity of the poverty estimates for 1985-86. First, the decrease in poverty observed for that year does not match consumption measures obtained from the national income accounts (Ravallion 1990). Moreover, the survey suffers from lower quality data than were available in other years. Thus, the drop in poverty observed for that year may be overestimated.

deploys variants of the cost of basic needs method. These studies indicate that both rural and urban poverty increased from the second half of the 1980s up to 1991-92 (Khandker, Mahmud, Sen, and Ahmed 1994; Hossain and Sen 1992; Ravallion and Sen 1996). They also find higher rural poverty than urban poverty throughout the late 1980s and up to 1991-92. In this report, access to the household-level HES data for estimating poverty measures has enabled more detailed results.

1.15   A second group of poverty studies is based on a series of small-scale surveys conducted by the Bangladesh Institute of Development Studies. This group shows an increase in poverty in the late 1980s, followed by a decrease in the 1990s (Rahman and Hossain 1995; Rahman, Hossain, and Sen 1996).

1.16   Estimates of poverty incidence by BBS using the direct calorie intake method show different results than those obtained with the cost of basic needs method (table 1.3). The two biggest differences relate to poverty trends in the 1990s and to rural-urban comparisons. *First,* the direct calorie intake method suggests that only rural poverty using the lower caloric threshold declined between 1991-92 and 1995-96; urban poverty incidence actually increased, particularly for the upper caloric threshold. Although the direct calorie intake estimates suggest that between 1983-84 and 1995-96 poverty declined more than indicated by the cost of basic needs estimates, the decline according to the direct calorie intake method occurred largely between 1983-84 and 1985-86, but according to the cost of basic needs method it declined primarily after 1991-92. *Second,* the cost of basic needs estimates consistently show that rural poverty is higher than urban poverty, whereas the direct calorie intake measures suggest that poverty rates are similar in rural and urban areas for most survey years. The food energy intake method gives results similar to the direct calorie intake estimates (because both rely on the actual caloric intake).[4]

Table 1.3: Headcount Indices of Poverty with the Direct Calorie Intake Method, 1983-84 to 1995-96
(percentage of population below the poverty line)

| | Lower caloric threshold | | | | | Upper caloric threshold | | | | |
| | 1,800 kcal | | 1,805 kcal | | | 2,200 kcal | | 2,122 kcal | | |
	1983-84	1985-86	1988-89	1991-92	1995-96	1983-84	1985-86	1988-89	1991-92	1995-96
National	36.8	26.9	28.4	28.0	25.1	62.6	55.7	47.8	47.5	47.5
Rural	36.7	26.3	28.6	28.3	24.6	61.9	54.7	47.8	47.6	47.1
Urban	37.4	30.7	26.4	26.3	27.3	67.7	62.6	47.6	46.7	49.7

Note: Part of the large decrease in poverty observed for the upper caloric threshold between 1985-86 and 1988-89 is due to the lowering of the caloric threshold for 1988-89 and after.
Source: BBS (1997e).

1.17   *Independent evidence on changes in living standards.* In addition to measures of poverty incidence, other independent evidence suggests that standards of living improved in the first half of the 1990s as reported by the cost of basic needs method. As noted by Mitchell (1998), Helen Keller International's National Surveillance Project report (Round 41) indicates that malnutrition in rural areas (as measured by the percentage of underweight children) since mid-1990 was at its lowest level in December 1996. The percentage of underweight children had declined by approximately 13 percent compared to August 1990. Also according to CIRDAP (1997c), real wages increased by about 7 percent between 1991-92 and 1996, especially in the agriculture and manufacturing sectors (this is discussed in

---

4 Several recent food energy intake measures of poverty are available in BBS reports related to a separate BBS Poverty Monitoring Project (BBS 1996a, 1997d). Unfortunately, the short horizon over which this project measures poverty reduces its value for analyzing long-term trends. The food energy intake estimates from this project are not always comparable to those obtained by the BBS using the full HES for previous years because of differences in survey methodologies and in the food energy intake method itself.

greater detail in chapter 3). And at a more aggregate level, the fact that GDP growth has consistently outpaced population growth over the last decade is consistent with a decrease in poverty over time.

Poverty has decreased the most in urban areas

1.18   The cost of basic needs headcount indexes (the method used for the rest of this report) suggest that poverty has declined in 1995-96 compared to 1983-84. How have changes in rural and urban poverty over time affected national poverty? A sectoral decomposition of the changes in national poverty incidence suggests that the rural sector, with 85 percent of the population, contributed only 47 percent of the total decrease in national poverty between 1983 and 1996 (Background Paper 11). The urban sector, with only 15 percent of the population, contributed 30 percent of the decline. Rural-to-urban migration accounted for 13 percent, and interaction effects the remaining 9 percent. The results of the decomposition are similar if only the last five years are used to measure this change.

The depth and severity of poverty are worse in rural areas

1.19   The poverty gap and squared poverty gap measures offer additional insights into poverty incidence. The poverty gap is the ratio of the average extra consumption needed to get all poor people to the poverty line, divided by the poverty line. It estimates how far below the poverty line the poor are on average as a proportion of that line (for the nonpoor the distance is zero). It also gives an idea of the minimum resources required to close the gap. The squared poverty gap takes into account not only the distance separating the poor from the poverty line, but also inequality among the poor (Foster, Greer, and Thorbecke 1984). The poverty gap is often interpreted as measuring the depth of poverty, and the squared poverty gap the severity of poverty.[5] Both measures confirm that rural poverty is much higher than urban poverty and suggest similar trends over time—stagnation in poverty during the 1980s and a decline in the 1990s (table 1.4).

Table 1.4: Poverty Gap and Squared Poverty Gap Measures of Poverty, 1983-84 to 1995-96

	Very poor (lower poverty line)					*Poor (upper poverty line)*				
	1983-84	*1985-86*	*1988-89*	*1991-92*	*1995-96*	*1983-84*	*1985-86*	*1988-89*	*1991-92*	*1995-96*
Poverty gap										
National	10.42	6.85	9.89	10.74	7.89	16.52	12.27	15.35	17.19	14.37
Rural	10.51	7.36	10.76	11.73	8.90	16.83	12.50	16.01	18.06	15.40
Urban	6.53	3.70	4.20	4.89	2.75	14.26	10.85	11.06	12.00	9.19
Squared poverty gap										
National	3.69	2.14	3.43	3.86	2.59	6.61	4.20	5.77	6.76	5.36
Rural	3.88	2.31	3.78	4.25	2.95	6.72	4.27	6.07	7.15	5.74
Urban	2.29	1.04	1.21	1.53	0.80	5.78	3.81	3.83	4.43	3.44

Note: Based on the cost of basic needs method.
Source: World Bank staff estimates. The 1995-96 estimates are also in BBS (1997e).

---

[5] The difficulty with using the headcount index rather than the poverty gap and the squared poverty gap can be illustrated with an example of two households with per capita consumption expenditures of Tk 400 and Tk 450 per month, respectively, in an area where the poverty line is Tk 500 per capita per month. If the first household receives a transfer of Tk 50 per person, the headcount ratio for the area will not change. If, instead, the second household receives the transfer, it will no longer be below the poverty line, and the headcount index will fall. The poverty gap will decrease by the same amount for both transfers. But the squared poverty gap will decrease more if the first household receives the transfer, because the squared poverty gap is distribution sensitive. Using the squared poverty gap as a poverty indicator will lead to better policy decisions. In contrast, the objective of lowering the headcount index would have the transfer go to the richest among the poor; the objective of lowering the poverty gap would be indifferent to which household received the transfer.

Inequality has grown

1.20   Has inequality increased or decreased nationally and within the rural and urban sectors? Inequality is higher in urban than in rural areas and has increased over time in both sectors, especially between 1991-92 and 1995-96 (figure 1.2a and Annex table 1.3). Urban inequality has increased much more than rural inequality. Decomposing the national Gini coefficient by sector indicates that the increase in the national Gini was due not only to rising inequality within sectors, but also to rising inequality between the urban and rural sectors (figure 1.2b). The between-sector component of the decomposition increased substantially, particularly between 1991-92 and 1995-96 (see Background Papers 8 and 11). The changes in stratification (a measure of the lack of overlap between the consumption levels of urban and rural households) also indicate larger differences in welfare over time between urban and rural households.

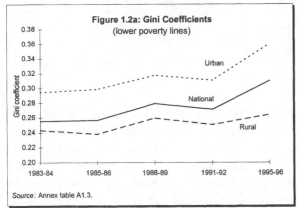

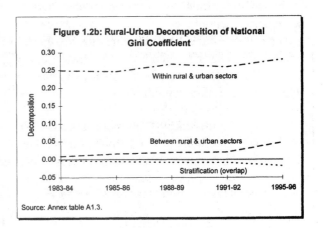

Note: The Gini index for real per capita consumption is defined as nominal per capita consumption deflated by the lower regional poverty lines taken to be the price index.

WHO ARE THE POOR?

1.21   Do the poor live mainly in rural or urban areas? Are they illiterate? Do they own land? Are households headed by women poorer than households headed by men? This section examines these and other characteristics of poor and very poor households.

Regions with large urban areas fare best

1.22   Urban households tend to be better off than rural households. But there are also large differences in the incidence of poverty between different regions and between urban and rural areas within those regions. The Dhaka, Chittagong, and Khulna administrative divisions have lower incidences of urban and rural poverty than the Barisal and Rajshahi divisions (Annex table A1.4). That is not surprising given the positive impact of large cities in the Dhaka, Chittagong, and Khulna divisions (the Dhaka and Chittagong Standard Metropolitan Areas have even lower headcount indexes). The contrast between urban and rural poverty incidence is the greatest for the Dhaka and Rajshahi divisions, the two divisions with positive net rural-to-urban migration according to the 1991 Census.

1.23   The proportion of the nation's poor living in each division or living in rural and urban areas can be computed using population shares. Ninety-three percent of the very poor and 89 percent of the poor live in rural areas. The Dhaka division, because of its large size, has the largest number of the very poor and the poor nationally and the largest number of the urban very poor and poor. The Rajshahi division has the largest number of the rural poor and very poor.

Social indicators are correlated with poverty

1.24   *Education.* Households whose heads did not have any education had a higher probability of being poor in 1995-96 (figure 1.3 and Annex table A1.5). Nationally, the headcount index for very poor households was 48 percent if headed by a person without any schooling and 7 percent if the head had completed the secondary school certificate and above. Using the upper poverty lines, 67 percent of household heads with no schooling were poor across the country, as compared to 16 percent of household heads who had completed the secondary school certificate and above. Poverty falls as the level of education of the household head rises, and it falls faster in urban than in rural areas, suggesting higher returns to education in urban areas.

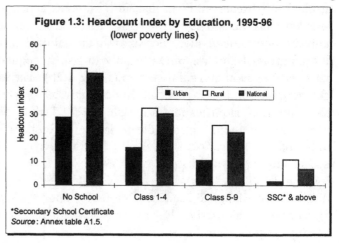

1.25   *Land ownership.* The more land that a household owned beyond half an acre, the less likely it was to be poor (figure 1.4 and Annex table A1.6). Owners of less than half an acre were the most likely to be poor—even more likely than landless households. While education had a strong impact in urban

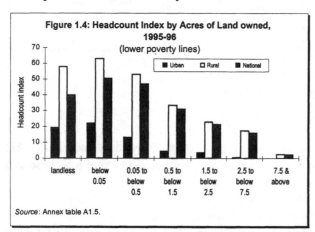

areas, land mattered the most in rural areas. Among the landless in rural areas, six of ten were very poor and seven of ten were poor. Among marginal landowners (owning less than half an acre), six of ten were very poor and eight of ten were poor. Only one in 40 was very poor among large rural landowners (owning at least 7.5 acres) and only one in ten was poor.

1.26   *Occupation of the household head.* In the rural sector owner-farmers have the lowest probability of being poor (20 percent with the lower poverty lines), followed by workers in nonagricultural activities (38 percent); tenant farmers (42 percent); workers in fisheries, forestry, and livestock (45 percent); agricultural workers with family land (51 percent); and agricultural workers without family land (75 percent) (see BBS 1997e). In the nonagricultural sector, most high-level employees (executives, officials, professionals, teachers) and most small businesspeople and petty traders escape poverty. Factory workers and artisans rank below them, followed by salespeople, service workers, and brokers, as well as transport and communications workers. Servants and day laborers have relatively higher poverty rates. Households in which the head is not working, including households headed by retired workers and students, do not fare badly, probably because they have other sources of income or support that allow the head not to work. Heads who have a second occupation tend to be in poorer households, suggesting that the second occupation is pursued out of necessity. An exception is households whose heads have a second occupation as an owner-farmer.

1.27   *Rural farm versus nonfarm workers.* There has been a debate in Bangladesh over the living standards of rural farm versus nonfarm workers (see World Bank 1997b). The traditional view has held that the bulk of nonfarm activities are residual, low-productivity occupations which the landless poor are pushed into. Therefore, the growth of the rural nonfarm sector is interpreted as a sign of weakness rather than strength in rural development. If that were the case, rural nonfarm workers would be employed in residual activities, receiving extremely low wages, and their poverty rates would be higher than those of rural agricultural landless households. But the 1995-96 HES shows that rural households whose heads are landless agricultural workers are the poorest. This finding supports the alternative view of the development of the nonfarm sector, which maintains that growth of the nonfarm sector pulls people out of poverty in rural areas. Promoting the rural nonfarm sector, including fisheries, livestock, and forestry (for example through microcredit programs) therefore represents an attractive policy option for reducing poverty in rural areas (see Background Paper 2).

1.28   *Gender disparities.* Rural households headed by women have a higher probability of being among the very poor than households headed by men (45 percent versus 39 percent), but not urban households (about 14 percent of both female-and male-headed urban households are very poor; see BBS 1997e for details). The headcount ratios for poor households are virtually identical for both female (52 percent) and male-headed (53 percent) households. To the extent that female-headed households have smaller families, and the use of per capita consumption as the welfare indicator underestimates poverty among smaller families compared to large families,[6] differences in poverty between female and male-headed households are likely to be larger. Further, if the distribution of consumption within households favors men, poverty among women is likely to be higher still.

1.29   While poverty is best measured by comparing per capita consumption to a poverty line, there are other dimensions of well-being that are not captured by such measures. Gender inequality is an important case in point, since women in Bangladesh lack access to health and education. Women have a lower life expectancy than men at birth. Moreover, in 1993 the ratio of female-to-male child mortality was 1.33, and the ratio of female-to-male children who received no treatment for episodes of fever or acute respiratory infection was 1.19 (Filmer, King, and Pritchett 1998). Bangladesh's gender performance in education is better: the ratio of female-to-male enrollment for children aged 11 to 14 was 0.93 in 1993, well above the South Asian median of 0.70. Yet, girls still lag behind boys, especially in secondary and higher education. Girls are not only less likely than boys to attend post-primary school, they are also less likely to complete school when they do attend. Moreover, women represent a small minority of teachers: 19 percent in primary education and only 10 percent in secondary education (World Bank 1996a).

1.30   *Attitudes toward women.* Attitudes toward women are an important social determinant of equity, access to public services, and women's well-being. The rural community module of the 1995-96 HES provides important information on village attitudes, of both men and women, toward women's participation in income-generating activities, education, and family planning. Men and women have different attitudes toward women taking up income-generating activities: in almost three-quarters of the villages most women favored or strongly favored doing so, but that view is held by a majority of men in less than half the villages (table 1.5). Support for female education is universally higher than support for income-generating activities and is more even between men and women. Support or strong support for female education is the majority view of men in 84 percent of villages and the majority view of women in 90 percent of villages. There are many villages (more than 20 percent) in which men oppose or strongly oppose women engaging in income-generating activities, but almost none where they oppose or strongly oppose women's education. Most men support or strongly support family planning for women in 56 percent of the villages; most women do so in 65 percent of the villages.

---

6 This is because per capita consumption as a welfare indicator does not take into account economies of scale within larger households, for example larger households need not spend as much on housing per capita as small households may have to.

Table 1.5: Village Attitudes toward Women, 1995-96
(percentage of villages with a majority view)

	Women's income-earning activities		Female education		Family planning	
	Men	*Women*	*Men*	*Women*	*Men*	*Women*
In favor	41.0	50.8	57.3	44.5	40.3	38.9
Strongly in favor	6.3	23.5	27.2	45.4	16.4	25.9
Opinion divided	29.7	10.5	12.6	7.1	33.6	20.9
Against	16.7	7.1	1.3	0.8	4.2	4.2
Strongly against	3.8	1.3	0.4	0.4	2.5	0.8
No opinion	2.5	6.7	1.3	1.7	2.9	9.2
All responses	100.0	100.0	100.0	100.0	100.0	100.0
Number of villages	239	238	239	238	238	239

Note: Shares are not weighted by village population. Percentages may not add up to 100 percent due to rounding or coding.
Source: World Bank staff estimates using 1995-96 HES.

1.31   *Marital status, age of household head, and household size.* Household heads who are unmarried are less likely to be poor than those who are married, and married household heads are less poor than widowed or divorced household heads (see BBS 1997e for details). Individuals living in households where the head was widowed or divorced had a higher incidence of poverty (43 percent) compared to the population as a whole (36 percent). There appears to be an "inverted U" relationship between poverty incidence and the age of the household head: poverty rises for households with heads up to 39 years old and declines thereafter. Poverty also increases with household size of up to six members and then declines, possibly because of the presence of additional adults with earning ability. But, the relationship between household size and poverty is contingent on the equivalence scale used for measuring consumption. By using per capita consumption as the indicator of well-being we do not take into account potential economies of scale within households, and therefore we may overestimate poverty among larger households as compared to smaller households.

1.32   A large number of other household and other characteristics can be related to poverty incidence (see BBS 1997e for examples). Instead of doing so here, the reader is referred to chapter 3, where the correlates of poverty are discussed in greater detail.[7]

COMPARING BANGLADESH TO SOUTH AND EAST ASIA

1.33   *Bangladesh compares well in some areas with its South Asian neighbors, but lags in nutrition, infant mortality, and literacy.* Bangladesh has a lower GNP per capita than all other South Asian countries except for Nepal (table 1.6). Population growth in Bangladesh is now lower than that in other South Asian countries except Sri Lanka, but labor force growth is similar, implying, as elsewhere, a need for rapid, labor-intensive economic growth. Bangladesh has a relatively high incidence of poverty measured by the headcount index.[8] Life expectancy at birth in Bangladesh is lower and child malnutrition higher than in other South Asian countries, except for Nepal. Infant mortality is higher except when compared to that in Nepal and Pakistan. Access to safe water in Bangladesh has been the best in South Asia (however, this is not taking into account the increasingly recognized problem of arsenic contamination of ground water in Bangladesh). Bangladesh lags behind in literacy, although gross

---

[7] We are also developing a simple spreadsheet model that allows a user to estimate the probability of being poor as a function of different combinations of household characteristics, such as education, land ownership, or occupation. This will allow a flexible representation of the poverty profile. This software will be available upon request.

[8] These comparisons should be treated with caution since each country uses different methodologies for measuring poverty.

primary school enrollment now is approaching 100 percent (in part because of over-age students and repeaters in primary schools) and has near gender parity.

Table 1.6: Bangladesh and South Asia: Comparisons of Selected Development Indicators, 1996 or Most Recent Estimates

	Bangladesh	India	Nepal	Pakistan	Sri Lanka	South Asia
Population mid-1996 *(millions)*	121.6	943.2	22.0	133.5	18.3	1264.0
GNP per capita 1996 *(US$)*	260	380	220	490	740	380
Poverty headcount index (% of population) [a]	36	35	42	34	22	na
Population growth *(%)*	1.6	1.7	2.5	2.9	1.3	1.9
Labor force growth *(%)*	2.1	2.0	2.4	3.3	2.0	2.1
Urban population *(% of total population)*	18	27	14	35	22	26
Life expectancy at birth *(years)*	58	62	55	60	72	61
Infant mortality *(per 1,000 live births)*	77	68	91	90	16	75
Child malnutrition *(% of children under 5)*	67	63	70	40	38	na
Access to safe water *(% of population)*	96	63	48	60	57	63
Illiteracy *(% of population age 15 & older)*	62	48	73	62	10	50
Gross primary enrollment *(% of school-age population)*	92	102	109	69	105	98

[a] Poverty estimates are based on different methodologies and should be used with caution. na = not available
Source: World Bank Economic and Social Database.

1.34   *East Asia suggests the possibilities for rapid growth and poverty reduction in Bangladesh.* Comparing Bangladesh with East Asian countries highlights the potential gains of growth and investment in human capital (table 1.7). Growth in East Asia has been associated not only with poverty reduction but also with rapid improvement of other social indicators (Ahuja and others 1997). For example, infant mortality in East Asia is half the rate in Bangladesh, and the illiteracy rate is one-third. Vietnam is the East Asian country closest to Bangladesh in terms of development indicators.

Table 1.7: Bangladesh and East Asia: Comparisons of Selected Development Indicators , 1996 or Most Recent Estimates

	Bangladesh	China	Indonesia	Philippines	Vietnam	Thailand	East Asia
Population mid-1996 *(millions)*	121.6	1211.3	196.1	70.0	75.3	58.7	1726.0
GNP per capita 1996 *(US$)*	260	750	1,090	1,190	290	3,020	890
Poverty headcount index *(% of population)* [a]	36	9	11	54	51	13	na
Population growth *(%)*	1.6	1.1	1.6	2.2	2.0	0.9	1.3
Labor force growth *(%)*	2.1	1.1	2.5	2.7	1.9	1.3	1.3
Urban population *(% of total population)*	18	30	36	54	21	20	31
Life expectancy at birth *(years)*	58	69	64	66	68	69	68
Infant mortality *(per 1,000 live births)*	77	34	51	39	41	35	40
Child malnutrition *(% of children under 5)*	67	17	11	30	45	13	na
Access to safe water *(% of population)*	96	46	63	84	38	81	49
Illiteracy *(% of population age 15 & older)*	62	19	16	5	6	6	17
Gross primary enrollment *(% of school-age population)*	92	109	115	111	114	87	117

[a] Poverty estimates are based on different methodologies and should be used with caution. na = not available.
Source: World Bank Economic and Social Database.

1.35   Comparing Bangladesh with Indonesia, also a predominantly rural and densely populated country, is especially revealing (figures 1.5a to 1.5d). Indonesia had a per capita GNP similar to Bangladesh's at the latter's Independence in 1971. The gap widened slightly in the mid-1970s and then sharply in the late 1980s. In 1996, prior to its recent currency crisis, Indonesia's GNP per capita was four times that of Bangladesh. The gaps between Indonesia and Bangladesh on the illiteracy rate, life expectancy at birth, and infant mortality have also widened over time.

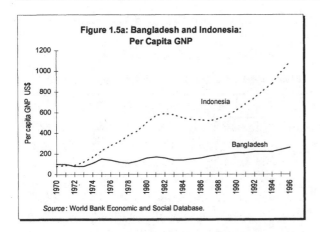

Figure 1.5a: Bangladesh and Indonesia: Per Capita GNP

Source: World Bank Economic and Social Database.

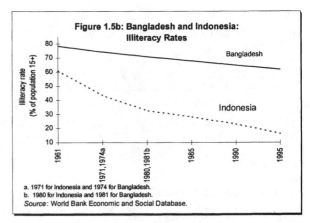

Figure 1.5b: Bangladesh and Indonesia: Illiteracy Rates

a. 1971 for Indonesia and 1974 for Bangladesh.
b. 1980 for Indonesia and 1981 for Bangladesh.
Source: World Bank Economic and Social Database.

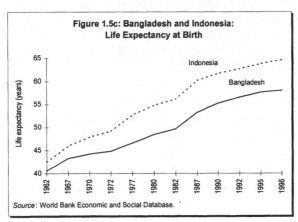

Figure 1.5c: Bangladesh and Indonesia: Life Expectancy at Birth

Source: World Bank Economic and Social Database.

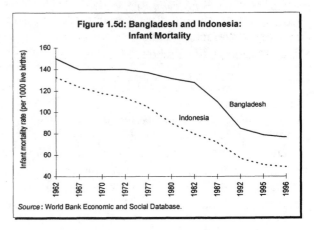

Figure 1.5d: Bangladesh and Indonesia: Infant Mortality

Source: World Bank Economic and Social Database.

SUMMARY

1.36   The World Bank had five objectives in launching its 1994 program to assist the BBS in building its capacity to improve the collection and analysis of poverty data:

- Enhance BBS's institutional capacity to field complex, integrated household surveys using modern techniques of data collection and entry.
- Help make the official methodology used for poverty measurement and monitoring more robust analytically so that it is well suited for comparisons over time and space.
- Help change the official BBS policy of granting limited or no access to the data for researchers.
- Help expand the focus of BBS and other poverty analysts beyond poverty measurement issues to poverty analysis that feeds into policy and program design.
- Prepare a poverty assessment.

The first three objectives have been achieved and are discussed here. The fourth objective—shifting attention away from measurement to policy issues—is being pursued as part of a long-term process of institutional development. This report meets the last objective.

1.37   Using the recommended cost of basic needs method for measuring poverty suggests that:

- The incidence of poverty has decreased significantly between 1991-92 and 1995-96, after stagnating over most of the 1980s.
- Rural poverty continues to dominate urban poverty, and the gap appears to be increasing. The incidence of poverty also varies considerably by region within the urban and rural sectors.
- Inequality has increased over the long term in both urban and rural areas.

1.38   The profile of the poor in 1995-96 suggests that:

- Higher levels of education and land ownership are associated with a lower probability of being poor.
- Rural households whose heads are employed in the nonfarm sector are less likely to be poor on average than landless households with heads working in the farm sector, and more likely to be poor than urban households with heads in the same occupations.
- Female-headed households are poorer than male-headed households in rural areas. Women lag behind in other dimensions of wellbeing, such as access to health and education.

1.39   Attitudes toward women are an important determinant of equity. Data from the 1995-96 HES suggests that support for women's education is universally higher than support for income-generating activities in rural villages and is more even between men and women. On the issue of women joining income-generating activities, a majority of men was in favor in 47 percent of villages, as compared to a majority of women in favor in 74 percent of the villages. Village support for female education was more even: a majority of women in 90 percent of villages and a majority of men in 84 percent of villages.

1.40   International comparisons show that despite recent progress, Bangladesh still lags behind other South and East Asian developing countries. For example, Indonesia has outperformed Bangladesh not only in per capita GNP growth, but also in life expectancy and in reducing infant mortality and illiteracy.

OVERVIEW OF CHAPTER 2. GROWTH, INEQUALITY, AND POVERTY

PARA.	KEY CONCLUSIONS	POLICY IMPLICATIONS
2.2 to 2.11	**Looking back: growth and inequality** From 1983 to 1996 the headcount ratio for the very poor fell from 41 to 36 percent. Poverty reduction has been slow partly because growth was associated with higher inequality. Depending on the poverty measure used, one-fifth to one-third of the potential decrease in poverty resulting from growth is estimated to have been lost because of rising inequality. The impact of rising inequality on poverty reduction has been especially strong in urban areas and much weaker in rural areas.	The higher inequality associated with growth in Bangladesh does not imply that growth should not be pursued. To the contrary, higher growth is needed if poverty is to be reduced faster. But given the risk of rising inequality, safety nets must be extended and pro-poor investments in human and physical capital made.
2.12 to 2.25	**Looking ahead: three growth scenarios** Using a macroeconomic consistency model, three simple hypothetical growth scenarios are examined to understand some of the implications of alternative growth patterns for poverty and inequality. These scenarios assume that the recent changes in inequality associated with growth will continue in the future. *Steadily accelerating growth* With GDP growth progressively rising to 7.3 percent in the decade ahead, poverty would be 13 percentage points lower in 2008 than in 1995-96. The decrease in poverty would be strongest in industry and services due to higher assumed growth in those sectors. This reference scenario is compared with two other scenarios. *Higher nonagricultural growth* This scenario is intended to illustrate the importance of aggregate saving and the financing of investment for faster growth. As a result of higher domestic saving (and lower consumption) needed to finance investment, somewhat higher growth (mainly in services, the conclusion would be the same for growth in industry), would result only in slightly lower poverty as compared to the reference scenario. To the extent that remittances (as part of national saving) or foreign saving finance investment and growth, and safety nets cover the poor so that their consumption is protected, poverty reduction would be that much greater. *Higher agricultural growth* This scenario is intended to illustrate the importance of changes in inequality with growth and the impact on poverty reduction. Assuming that the recent pattern of growth and inequality persists over the next decade, faster growth from agriculture would contribute to inequality less and reduce poverty incidence more.	Faster growth from industry, services, and agriculture is required simultaneously to reduce poverty faster and further. Sound macroeconomic management and policy reforms leading to faster economic growth should help. To finance the investment needed for higher growth without reducing domestic consumption substantially, foreign investment must increase and aid utilization must improve. Economic growth from industry and services has outstripped agricultural growth and will continue to make an increasing contribution to poverty reduction. However, given the size of the agricultural economy, and assuming the recent experience of growth and inequality continues, higher growth in agriculture would also help to reduce poverty incidence and dampen the increase in inequality. Such growth can come from intensification of rice cultivation and the diversification into other nonfood crops. It is also possible that the impact of growth on poverty may change in the future. For example, the greater difficulty of reaching the poorest in the rural sector through growth may lower the impact of agricultural growth on poverty reduction. On the other hand, rising demand for labor and employment as a result of faster industrial growth may serve to increase the impact of growth on poverty reduction.

CHAPTER 2: GROWTH, INEQUALITY, AND POVERTY

2.1   Bangladesh's economic growth has exceeded its population growth, especially since the early 1990s. GDP growth has averaged around 4 percent over the past 12 years, and was 4.4 percent during 1991 to 1997, whereas the population growth rate was about 2 percent. This should have resulted in increased consumption and reduced poverty. Yet poverty declined slowly, with no net gains between 1983 and 1992. Rural poverty in particular remains very high, and the number of the poor has increased over time. Why has poverty declined so slowly?

LOOKING BACK: GROWTH IN AVERAGE CONSUMPTION AND INEQUALITY

2.2   From 1983 to 1996 the national headcount index of poverty fell from 40.9 to 35.6 percent using the lower poverty lines, and from 58.5 to 53.1 percent using the upper poverty lines. Part of the answer to why poverty declined so slowly lies in rising inequality during this period.

Growth lowered poverty, but inequality increased it, especially in urban areas

2.3   As noted in chapter 1, inequality was higher in the urban than in the rural sector, and increased over time in both sectors, especially between 1991-92 and 1995-96. Figure 2.1 (and Annex table A2.1) shows a simulation of what the national headcount ratio (using the lower poverty lines—the results are similar for the upper poverty lines) would have been with the actual pattern of growth in per capita consumption but without changes in inequality (the "growth" headcount line). Poverty would have been about 10 percentage points lower in 1995-96 than what was actually observed (see Background Paper 9). What impact did rising per capita consumption and inequality have on poverty incidence in the rural and urban sectors? The simulation shown in figure 2.1 can be carried out for each sector separately (Annex table A2.1). Using the lower poverty lines, and factoring out the increase in inequality, poverty would have been 5 percentage points lower in rural areas and 6 points lower in urban areas in 1995-96.[1]

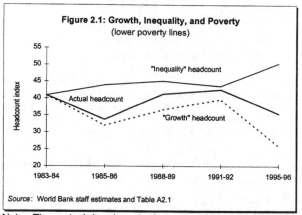

Figure 2.1: Growth, Inequality, and Poverty
(lower poverty lines)

Source: World Bank staff estimates and Table A2.1

Note: The actual headcount shows the observed national headcount indexes; the "growth" headcount shows the headcount index simulated with the actual growth in per capita consumption but assuming no change in inequality; the "inequality" headcount shows the headcount index simulated with the actual rise in inequality but assuming no growth in per capita consumption.

One-fifth of the potential poverty reduction from growth was lost due to rising inequality

2.4   The above simulations take into account actual changes in growth and inequality, but they do not tell us much about the relationship between growth and inequality. To better quantify their relationship and its implications for poverty, we created a regional panel—comprising cross-sectoral and time-series variables—with welfare measures (mean consumption, poverty, and inequality) for the 14 areas and the five survey years between 1983-84 and 1995-96 (see Background Paper 9).

---

[1]   The "inequality" headcount line shows a "no-growth" situation of the impact of actual changes in inequality on poverty incidence but without any growth in per capita consumption: poverty in 1995-96 would then have been 15 points higher nationally, 8 percentage points higher in rural areas, and 24 percentage points higher in urban areas than actually observed.

2.5   Nationally, without the rise in inequality, a one percentage point increase in per capita consumption would have resulted in a 2.42 percentage point decline in the headcount ratio (using the lower poverty line) (table 2.1). With a headcount of about 40 percent, this represents a one percentage point decline in the share of the population below the poverty line. Growth in per capita consumption and rising inequality are also correlated—the elasticity of inequality with respect to growth is 0.35. Finally, rising inequality results in a rising headcount ratio—a one percentage point increase in the Gini coefficient of inequality increases the headcount index by 1.28 percentage points. The net elasticity of poverty with respect to growth is therefore -1.98 (as compared to the gross elasticity of -2.42). One-fifth of the potential decrease in poverty from growth was lost because inequality rose. The upper poverty lines show a similar but smaller loss.

Table 2.1: Elasticities of the Headcount Index with Respect to Growth and Inequality, 1983-84 to 1995-96

	National	*Rural*	*Urban*
Lower poverty lines			
Gross elasticity of poverty with respect to growth	-2.42	-2.20	-2.84
Elasticity of inequality with respect to growth	0.35	0.18	0.43
Elasticity of poverty with respect to inequality	1.28	0.88	2.10
Net elasticity of poverty with respect to growth	-1.98	-2.04	-1.95
Upper poverty lines			
Gross elasticity of poverty with respect to growth	-1.43	-1.23	-1.70
Elasticity of inequality with respect to growth	0.27	0.07	0.37
Elasticity of poverty with respect to inequality	0.52	0.29	0.92
Net elasticity of poverty with respect to growth	-1.29	-1.21	-1.33

Note: The net elasticity of poverty is the gross elasticity of poverty with respect to growth plus the product of the elasticity of inequality with respect to growth and the elasticity of poverty with respect to inequality. The estimates use a fixed effects model on a panel of welfare measures at the regional level. Estimates are similar with random effects. The gross impact of growth alone on poverty is the impact of holding inequality (as measured by the Gini coefficient) constant.
Source: World Bank staff estimates.

The association between growth and rising inequality is stronger in urban than in rural areas

2.6   The rural and urban estimates of these elasticities suggest an important difference that is not evident from the national figures: growth in per capita consumption has been associated with rising inequality in urban areas but not in rural areas. In urban areas the relationship was significant (the elasticities of inequality with respect to growth for the lower and upper poverty lines, 0.43 and 0.37, are statistically different from zero at the 5 percent level). In rural areas the relationship, although also positive, was much weaker (the elasticities for the lower and upper poverty lines, 0.18 and 0.07, are not statistically significant). Growth in rural per capita consumption therefore has a bigger net impact on reducing poverty under the lower poverty line than growth in urban per capita consumption.

2.7   The loss in poverty reduction due to rising inequality is stronger if poverty measures that are more sensitive to inequality are used. Nationally, using the lower poverty lines, the poverty gap measure suggests a net elasticity of poverty with respect to growth of -2.67 (instead of -3.47 when no change in inequality is assumed), so that one-fourth of the gains from growth are lost because of higher inequality (table 2.2). Using the squared poverty gap measure the net elasticity is -3.30 (instead of -4.39), so that one-third of the gains from growth are lost because of higher inequality.

2.8   The net elasticity of rural poverty with respect to growth is larger than the net elasticity of urban poverty with respect to growth in all but one case (the exception is the upper poverty lines and the headcount ratio). These results suggest that more rapid rural development will reduce poverty faster than more rapid urban development (see Background Paper 9 for details).

**Table 2.2: Net Elasticities of Poverty with Respect to Growth Using Alternative Poverty Measures,
1983-84 to 1995-96**

	Lower poverty lines			Upper poverty lines		
	National	*Rural*	*Urban*	*National*	*Rural*	*Urban*
Headcount	-1.98	-2.04	-1.95	-1.29	-1.21	-1.33
Poverty gap	-2.67	-3.08	-2.47	-2.17	-2.55	-1.96
Squared poverty gap	-3.30	-3.85	-3.05	-2.85	-3.50	-2.51

Note: The estimates use a fixed effect model on a panel of welfare measures at the regional level. Estimates are similar with random effects. The net impact of growth on poverty is the impact after accounting for the increase in inequality associated with growth.
Source: World Bank staff estimates.

Rising inequality in the short to medium term is not unusual, but a long-term rise would be unusual
2.9   Is Bangladesh's increase in inequality unusual compared to other countries? Kuznets (1955, 1963) and Oshima (1963) suggested in their inverted-U hypothesis that inequality widens in the initial phase of growth and then narrows. They perceived economic development to be a fundamentally sequential and uneven process, pulling up certain groups first and leaving other groups to catch up later. Despite its intuitive simplicity, the Kuznets hypothesis has not received clear-cut empirical support, in part because of a number of measurement problems with international, cross-section data. New international evidence using panel data does not suggest a simple, systematic, inverted-U relationship between growth and inequality when country-specific effects are controlled for (Deininger and Squire 1996; Bruno, Ravallion, and Squire 1996).

2.10   During the transition from an economically backward to a progressive sector, technical change, migration, saving behavior, and asset and labor markets may all increase inequality (Ray 1998). Eventually, as the transition is completed, less inequality will more likely prevail. Note that these uneven and compensatory changes occur not just in developing countries, but in industrial countries as well[2]. Thus the increase in inequality in Bangladesh would not be an exception over the short to medium term. However, a long-term trend of rising inequality would be relatively unusual. Only in a few semirural economies such as China, in Thailand and in several developed countries such as the United Kingdom, United States, and New Zealand has growth and rising inequality been correlated over long periods of time (Bruno, Ravallion, and Squire 1996). These considerations suggest that we need to better understand both the likely implications of alternative growth patterns in Bangladesh (discussed below) and the microeconomic determinants of inequality (discussed in chapter 3), so that public policies may help to reduce inequality over time.

LOOKING AHEAD: POVERTY AND GROWTH IN AGRICULTURE, INDUSTRY, AND SERVICES

2.11   How would different sectoral patterns of growth affect poverty? How does the saving required to finance investment affect poverty? To address these questions and to simulate future trends in poverty, we combine estimates from household level data with a macroeconomic consistency model.

Simulating the impact of sectoral growth patterns on poverty
2.12   The simulations in this section are not intended to provide forecasts of poverty reduction, since they do not take into account the many dynamic forces that can affect economic growth, inequality, and poverty. Rather, their objective is to approximate outcomes within a consistent macroeconomic framework to illustrate the tradeoffs and policy choices in promoting growth and poverty reduction.

---

[2] An example is the recent upsurge in inequality in the United States while its industrial structure is undergoing a transition.

2.13   In our model the impact of growth in agriculture, industry, and services on poverty depends on four parameters: the rate of sectoral population growth, the rate of sectoral GDP growth, the change over time in the share of sectoral GDP used for consumption, and the sectoral elasticity of poverty with respect to consumption growth.[3] First, we use data from the two most recent HES surveys (1991-92 and 1995-96) to estimate the net elasticities of poverty (using the lower poverty lines) with respect to per capita consumption growth in agriculture, industry, and services (table 2.3). These elasticities incorporate the observed correlation between growth and inequality. For example, a 1 percent increase in growth of per capita consumption of agricultural households generates a 1.67 percent decrease in the headcount index in agriculture. The corresponding sectoral elasticities for industry and services are -1.26 and -1.25. The difference in the size of the elasticities between agriculture and the other two sectors is the largest using the squared poverty gap. Inequality rises less in agriculture, so the squared poverty gap measure declines more with growth in agriculture than elsewhere. A possible explanation for lower inequality with growth in agriculture is that the wage structure is much more flat and hence the premium on skills is lower and growth yields more evenly distributed gains in the labor market. The higher growth elasticities in agriculture compared to industry and services reiterate our earlier finding—agricultural growth will reduce poverty more than the same industrial and service growth, and the difference will be larger using the poverty gap and squared poverty gap measures than the headcount index. For the sake of simplicity, we assume for our projections that these growth elasticities remain unchanged over time.

Table 2.3: Net Sectoral Elasticities of Poverty with Respect to Growth, 1991-92 to 1995-96

(using lower poverty lines and adjusting with respect to rise in inequality)

	Headcount	Poverty gap	Squared poverty gap
Agriculture	-1.67	-3.07	-4.22
Industry	-1.26	-2.36	-3.20
Services	-1.25	-1.91	-2.13

Note: These elasticities are for the most recent period, 1991-92 to 1995-96, during which inequality increased the most. They are therefore lower than the long-term elasticities reported in table 2.2. The more recent elasticities are used for the projections because they reflect the latest information and because they generate conservative projections of poverty reduction.

Source: World Bank staff estimates.

2.14   In addition to different sectoral growth paths, the saving required for higher growth will itself affect poverty over time. Higher economic growth requires higher investment, which should be financed through a higher national saving (domestic saving, and net current transfers and net factor income) and (or) through higher foreign saving in terms of capital inflows of aid, loans, or foreign investments. If the domestic saving rate is to rise, the share of GDP allocated to consumption must fall. And, assuming this increase in saving is uniform across the income distribution, higher growth would have a lower short-term impact on poverty.[4] Households would be exchanging current gains in consumption (and thus in poverty reduction) for future benefits. By contrast, if investment were financed in part by foreign saving, consumption as a share of GDP need not decrease as much, and the immediate impact of GDP growth on poverty would be larger (but if the financing is through loans, debts would have to be repaid later).

---

[3] The percentage change in per capita consumption in each sector following growth in average income is the sum of the growth rate of the share of income that is consumed and the growth rate of income per capita in that sector. The rate of change in the poverty measure is the sectoral growth elasticity of the measure (factoring in any changes in distribution) multiplied by the percentage change in per capita sectoral consumption. We estimate this rate for each sector. Using changing sectoral population shares over time to reflect different growth patterns by sector, we can then simulate changes in national poverty following changes in sectoral growth, consumption, and population.

[4] If the increase in domestic saving needed to finance growth comes from greater saving by better-off households rather than from saving and reductions in the consumption of the poor or very poor, then the impact of growth on poverty reduction would be that much greater.

Growth and poverty reduction scenarios

2.15 We examine three simple scenarios—one with steadily accelerating growth, one with higher growth coming from services, and one with higher growth coming from agriculture. We use a macroeconomic consistency model to estimate the investment needed to achieve various levels of growth and to finance the investment through the saving of households, the government, and the rest of the world.[5]

2.16 *Poverty would decline substantially under a 10-year scenario with steadily accelerating growth.* In the initial scenario GDP growth is projected to increase progressively to reach 7.3 percent per year by 2008, working out to an average growth rate of 6 percent over 1997-2008. This rate is higher than the 4.4 percent average growth rate observed in the past six years, but below the 7.3 percent target average rate projected in the Fifth Five-Year Plan for 1997-2002 (in that Plan growth increases from 5.7 percent in 1996-97 to 8.54 percent in 2001-2002).

2.17 GDP growth in this scenario would be expected to come primarily from industry and services rather than from agriculture. The scenario assumes a 2 percent growth rate in value added for agriculture each year. This figure corresponds to average climatic conditions. For industry, growth in value added would increase progressively from 3.6 percent in 1997 to 8.5 percent per year after 2004. The annual growth rate for services would increase from 6.2 to 7.5 percent.

2.18 Given limited availability of foreign financing, private consumption as a share of GDP would be expected to decline nationally by four percentage points, from 85.7 percent of GDP to 81.6 percent, in order to help finance investment. Since agricultural growth is limited, the share of GDP that agricultural households use for consumption is assumed to remain constant at the original national average. Consumption as a share of GDP in industry and services must thus decline more than the national average.

2.19 Overall, population growth is set at 1.5 percent per year until 2001 and at 1.2 percent thereafter until 2008. With rural-urban migration and occupational shifts, population growth is assumed to be higher in industry and services (at 2.25 percent until 2001, and at 1.8 percent thereafter) than in agriculture (0.75 and 0.6 percent). We can then derive sectoral growth rates in per capita consumption for each year from the model. Using the elasticities of poverty with respect to consumption growth then yields sectoral poverty projections (figure 2.2 and Annex table A2.2). The national headcount projections are obtained by tracking the population share in each sector over time.

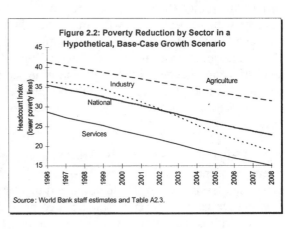

Figure 2.2: Poverty Reduction by Sector in a Hypothetical, Base-Case Growth Scenario

Source: World Bank staff estimates and Table A2.3.

2.20 In this reference scenario, poverty will decrease in all three sectors, with the largest decreases in industry and services because of their higher growth (which more than compensates for the higher sectoral population growth and the drop in the average propensity to consume in these two sectors). The national headcount index would fall from 35.6 percent (1995-96) to 22.9 percent (2008). This decline of

---

[5] Using a Leontief-type production function in which labor is abundant and capital is rationed, the World Bank's RMSM-X model assumes a relatively stable relationship between current investment and future GDP growth. The model also includes detailed monetary, budgetary, trade, pricing, and debt information. The general assumptions and economic reasoning behind the RMSM-X model are outlined in Easterly (1989) and Khan, Montiel, and Haque (1990). For recent use of the Bangladesh RMSM-X model and its underlying assumptions, see World Bank (1997a). Here the model assumes overall macroeconomic stability and no adverse macroeconomic shocks.

more than one-third is only slightly more than half the squared poverty gap decline of 60 percent (from 2.6 to 1.0), indicating that growth would not leave the worst off behind even though inequality may be rising over this period. On the other hand, if consumption as a share of GDP in agriculture were to decline to finance investment in other sectors, the poverty impact could be smaller (because the elasticity of poverty with respect to consumption growth is assumed to remain higher in agriculture). Other complications could include an increase over time in the elasticity of poverty with respect to growth— faster industrial growth would increase the demand of labor and bring upward pressure on real wages, thereby increasing the impact of such growth on poverty reduction.

2.21   *Faster nonagricultural growth would reduce poverty further, but the financing of investment needed for faster growth would be important.* The second scenario serves to illustrate the importance of how the investment needed to increase growth will be financed. The scenario assumes that the agricultural growth rate is unchanged at 2 percent, but assumes higher growth coming essentially from services (which has grown the fastest in recent years; the conclusions would be the same if growth were to come from industry rather than services), yielding average GDP growth in the next ten years closer to the 7.3 percent average growth rate projected by the government in its Fifth Five-Year Plan for 1997-2002. Under this higher-growth scenario poverty in agriculture does not change, since none of the assumptions for agriculture have changed. As expected, poverty falls only marginally compared to the reference scenario by the end of the period (less than one percentage point greater decline in the headcount index with the lower poverty lines) because of the higher saving rate necessary to maintain the higher investment (assuming the additional saving is generated by these two sectors only and not from additional foreign saving). To the extent that remittances (as part of national saving) or foreign saving through grants, aid, and loans finance investment and growth, and safety nets cover the poor so that their consumption is protected, poverty reduction would be that much greater.

2.22   *Faster growth from agriculture would reduce poverty more.* The third scenario serves to illustrate the importance of how inequality is associated with growth. The scenario is based on higher growth from agriculture rather than from services or industry. Given our assumption of unchanged elasticities of poverty with respect to growth, and given the size of the agricultural economy and the much greater incidence of poverty, promoting agriculture will clearly reduce poverty more than the second scenario. This scenario assumes an annual growth rate in this sector of 3.5 percent for 1997-2008. The aggregate level of saving needed is the same as in the second scenario. The difference in saving between the two scenarios is that in this (pro-agriculture) case, all sectors (including agriculture) contribute to the higher saving necessary for growth, because all sectors need to invest more to grow at a higher rate than in the past.

2.23   Under this scenario the national headcount would be 2.6 percentage points lower than in the reference scenario at the end of the decade. In other words, the headcount would have fallen by slightly more than ten percent by 2008 compared to what it would have been under the reference scenario. And this relative gain is higher for the squared poverty gap. This difference is due to the higher elasticity of poverty with respect to growth in agriculture when poverty is measured with the squared poverty gap. Finally, the level of inequality nationally would be lower in 2008 under this scenario than under the reference scenario because the between-group component of inequality (with groups defined by occupation) would be lower, and growth would have been associated with a smaller rise in inequality due to agricultural growth.

2.24   What do these simulations suggest for policy? *First*, if economic growth accelerates, we can expect significant poverty reduction, even after taking into account the potential impact of rising inequality. *Second*, to the extent that Bangladesh makes better use of the concessional foreign aid that it has access to, the impact of higher growth on poverty would be larger. And to the extent that safety nets better protect the consumption of the poorest, the impact of faster growth on poverty would be greater. *Third*, growth based on faster agricultural growth would bring additional gains in poverty reduction, and reduce inequality.

2.25 As a practical matter, to reduce poverty faster and further, faster growth from industry, services, and agriculture is required simultaneously. Sound macroeconomic management and policy reforms leading to faster economic growth should help. To finance the investment needed for higher growth without reducing domestic consumption substantially, foreign investment must increase and aid utilization must improve. Economic growth from industry and services has outstripped agricultural growth and will continue to make an increasing contribution to poverty reduction. However, given the size of the agricultural economy, and assuming the recent experience of growth and inequality continues, higher growth in agriculture would also help to reduce poverty incidence and dampen the increase in inequality. Such growth can come from intensification of rice cultivation and the diversification into other nonfood crops. It is also possible that the impact of growth on poverty will change in the future. For example, rising demand for labor as a result of faster industrial growth would serve to increase the impact of growth on poverty reduction. Similarly, the greater difficulty of reaching the poorest through growth in the rural sector may lower the impact of agricultural growth on poverty reduction.

SUMMARY

2.26 Economic growth has reduced poverty substantially in Bangladesh, but it has also been associated with higher inequality. Thus to achieve faster poverty reduction, the country must:
- Maintain pro-growth macroeconomic fundamentals that support higher growth and investment, and support measures preventing further rises in inequality, such as improvements in safety nets.
- Invest in the human capital of the poor so that they will not be left behind by growth.
- Make more effective use of concessional aid flows to spur sustainable growth and finance high-priority public programs that reduce poverty directly.

2.27 Future work should look at how initially high inequality affects the poor's ability to benefit from growth and the policy implications that follow from this:
- The elasticity of poverty to growth argument suggests that with higher initial inequality, the poor share less in the benefits of growth, and therefore are less likely to escape poverty through growth.
- The induced-growth argument suggests that higher initial inequality (or poverty) may result in lower subsequent growth, and therefore lower poverty reduction. The impact of inequality (or poverty) on future growth could be due, for example, to distortions from redistributive policies implemented to reduce inequality (or poverty) or to access to credit concentrated in the hands of a privileged few, which prevents the poor from investing.

2.28 There are other macroeconomic issues of interest that have not been discussed in this chapter. Chief among them is the labor market and its impact on wages and employment. While unemployment is low, underemployment is a nagging concern for one-third of the working population according to the BBS Labor Force Surveys. Policies for improving labor market performance could include:
- Using variants of current microcredit programs to increase employment opportunities, not just through self-employment but also through wage employment.
- Promoting occupational shifts in rural areas from the farm to the nonfarm sector.
- Encouraging the participation of women in the labor force and promoting changes in the attitudes of both men and women toward such participation.
- Improving access to education, which raises earnings and consumption.
- Furthering the cost-effective use of public works programs, such as Food for Work, to help the rural poor make a living in slack seasons while maintaining much needed infrastructure.

OVERVIEW OF CHAPTER 3: MICROECONOMIC DETERMINANTS OF POVERTY

PARA.	KEY CONCLUSIONS	POLICY IMPLICATIONS
3.4 to 3.6	**Returns to education** Holding other household characteristics constant, for a household whose head completes primary school, consumption rises 19 percent per capita in urban areas and 7 percent in rural areas compared to a household whose head has had no education. For secondary school, the gain is 48 percent in urban areas and 17 percent in rural areas. The gains are high for spouses as well. These figures have been relatively stable since 1983 and have increased for women.	The gains from education have remained high, despite recent increases in unemployment among the better educated, warranting greater investment in education. The increasing gains from education for spouses in rural households may denote greater participation of women in income-generating activities.
3.7 to 3.16	**Returns to land ownership, occupation, demographics, wages, and employment** Landlessness increases the probability of being poor, as do certain occupations. In agriculture, owner-farmers are the best off, followed by tenant farmers; workers in fisheries, forestry, and livestock; and agricultural workers with land. In industry and services, businesspeople, petty traders, and high-level employees are the most likely to escape poverty. Factory workers, artisans, salespeople, service workers, brokers, and transportation workers all fare better than landless agricultural workers. Real wages have increased, but agricultural wages have lagged behind manufacturing and national average wages. While unemployment is relatively low, underemployment remains high, especially in rural areas. Unemployment tends to be higher for those who are better educated. Households with many children tend to be poorer, but if there are large economies of scale in household consumption, larger households need not be poorer.	Given potential political and administrative constraints to land redistribution, promoting the nonfarm sector, microcredit programs, and human capital investment is a good strategy to raise the standards of living of landless agricultural workers. Nonfarm-related investments in the poorest regions would reduce poverty the most, although the absolute gains in per capita consumption from joining the nonfarm sector may be larger in better-off regions. The slower rise in agricultural wages is consistent with the slower decline in the incidence of rural poverty. Policies should be implemented to reduce underemployment in rural areas, for example by providing better opportunities for women.
3.17 to 3.22	**Area determinants of poverty** Differences in poverty between geographic areas depend more on different area characteristics than on differences in the characteristics of households located in these areas. Dhaka's advantage over other districts has increased over time.	Policies targeting investments to poor regions should be supported. These could include investments in rural roads and bridges, marketing facilities, health and school facilities, energy, and telecommunications.
3.23 to 3.24	**Determinants of inequality** In urban areas education contributes the most to inequality, while land ownership drives inequality the most in rural areas. In both urban and rural areas, location is the second largest determinant of inequality. Occupation has a lesser impact.	Enabling the poor to complete primary education is inequality-reducing, as is investing in poorer regions and eliminating land-labor market failures that further skew rural land distribution. Transfer and skill-building programs such as Food for Work and Vulnerable Group Development reduce inequality.

CHAPTER 3: MICROECONOMIC DETERMINANTS OF POVERTY

3.1   In addition to broad-based economic growth, investments in the poor's human and physical capital are widely recognized to reduce poverty. Which investments should have priority? Should the government invest in education, infrastructure, or both? Should microcredit programs be encouraged? In addition to human capital investments, should investments also be made to improve areas where the poor live? In this chapter we provide answers to these questions by presenting estimates of the returns to education, land ownership, geographical location, occupation, and demographic characteristics. We also look at how these returns have changed over time. The next section looks at education, occupational choice, labor markets (including trends in wages), land ownership, and demographics. The third section discusses the impact of area-specific characteristics, and the final section discusses the determinants of inequality.

ANALYZING THE DETERMINANTS OF POVERTY

3.2   *Regression models are better for analyzing poverty determinants.* Although tabulations of the incidence of poverty by household characteristics such as those provided in chapter 1 are useful, they do not necessarily identify the determinants of poverty. For example, poverty and a given household characteristic may appear to be correlated, but in fact, they may not be correlated with each other, but with a third variable. Simple tabulations also do not tell us much about the relative importance of different characteristics that may affect living standards. Are people poor mainly because they lack education or because they do not own land? Does the probability of being poor depend on where people live? More fundamentally, does poverty in Bangladesh depend primarily on the characteristics of households, or on the characteristics of the geographical regions where households are located?

3.3   We use a regression model to explore how household and regional characteristics determine real per capita consumption for each of the five HES survey years between 1983 and 1996 (for estimation details see Background Paper 11).[1] These estimates can be interpreted as the gains from (or returns to) a specific household characteristic, holding other characteristics constant, so that in some sense they are the "pure" gains in household per capita consumption from that characteristic.[2] We estimate separate regressions for urban and rural areas. Apart from household characteristics, the regressions include geographical identifiers that capture differences among "greater districts" (the former administrative entities under the division level), leaving the household variables to account for differences in real consumption levels within districts.[3] We also use the regression model to assess the impact that household characteristics have on inequality in per capita consumption.

---

[1] As noted in chapter 2, we are also developing easy-to-use spreadsheet models based on these regressions that allows users to estimate the probability of being poor as a function of different combinations of household characteristics.

[2] In the regressions the dependent variable measures real consumption by the logarithm of per capita consumption normalized by the lower regional poverty line to take into account differences in cost of living between areas. Normalizing by the upper poverty lines gives similar results.

[3] Although regressions represent an improvement over simple tabulations of poverty incidence by household characteristics, the relationships observed between the explanatory variables and per capita consumption need not imply causality: only the strength of the association is being measured. Yet the choice of the explanatory variables often makes causality plausible. For example, the education of the head and spouse can be considered determinants of consumption while that of children cannot, in the sense that the education of children depends more on standards of living than standards of living depend on the education of children.

Education improves well being substantially, and its impact continues to be high over time

3.4   *Consumption gains from education are very large.* Education has been shown to be closely associated with improved standards of living (Psacharopoulos 1994). Researchers usually measure the returns to education through wage or earnings equations estimated at the individual level. But in Bangladesh, where formal labor markets coexist with a great deal of informal labor participation and many households rely on self-employment, earnings equations may not be representative of the population as a whole. We use an alternative method here that measures the impact of the household head's educational attainment and, separately, that of the spouse, on per capita consumption at the household level. Holding all other household characteristics constant, we compare these per capita gains to the per capita consumption associated with the household of an uneducated household head or spouse. (Our estimates control for occupation; see Background Paper 10 for details and additional estimates of the gains from education with occupation considered as endogenous.) These relative per capita gains from education are very large: they varied in 1995-96 from 3 percent for an urban household with a spouse who had some primary education

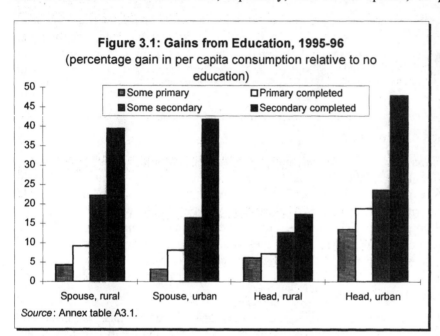

Figure 3.1: Gains from Education, 1995-96
(percentage gain in per capita consumption relative to no education)

Source: Annex table A3.1.

to 48 percent for an urban household with a head who had completed secondary school (figure 3.1 and Annex table A3.1).[4] Furthermore, these gains are additive: an urban household whose head and spouse have both completed secondary school would have an expected per capita consumption that is 90 percent greater than a similar household whose head and spouse have no schooling. Similarly, a rural household whose head and spouse have both completed secondary school would enjoy 57 percent higher per capita consumption.

3.5   *Average household consumption gains from the spouse's education are high.* The effects of education on per capita consumption are greater for urban households when it is the household head who is educated. But, for rural households the gains are generally greater when it is the spouse who is educated. The difference between the gains from secondary education for rural households that are attributable to the household head (17 percent) and to the spouse (39 percent) is particularly large.

3.6   *The large gains from education have persisted over time.* Between 1983-84 and 1995-96 the gains from education of the household head remained relatively stable, increasing slightly in urban areas and decreasing in rural areas (Annex table A3.1). Per capita consumption gains related to the spouse's education have also remained stable over time in urban areas and increased in rural areas. Yet these changes have been generally small—not surprisingly, though, since the proportion of households in

---

[4] The impact of education on the probability of being poor is directly proportional to the relative percentage gains shown in figure 3.1—the higher is the gain, the lower is the probability of being poor.

different education groups has been relatively stable (the increase in primary and secondary enrollment over the past 15 years has not yet changed the education levels of household heads and spouses). If the proportion of household heads who completed primary school had increased dramatically, the gains from education might have fallen because of the additional pressure on wage markets for adult primary school graduates. This has not been observed in urban areas, where wage markets are likely to be deeper and more developed, though in rural areas, where many household heads are self-employed, the gains have declined slightly over time. The increasing gains for spouses in rural areas may result from women's increasing participation in income-generating activities. The persistence of these high consumption gains from education, and the as yet small changes in these gains over time from rising educational attainment suggest that these gains can be expected to remain high, warranting further investment in education.

Certain occupations are associated with poverty

3.7   *Returns to occupation vary considerably, but landless agricultural workers fare the worst.* To calculate returns to a particular occupation, we measured the per capita consumption of households whose head is working in one of various agricultural and nonagricultural occupations relative to the consumption level of a landless agricultural worker (and controlling for other household characteristics). Among agricultural occupations in 1995-96, rural households with owner-farmers as heads enjoyed the highest per capita consumption (23 percent higher than that of households headed by a landless agricultural worker); followed by tenant farmers (18 percent higher); workers in fisheries, forestry, and livestock (16 percent higher); and agricultural workers with family land (11 percent higher, figure 3.2a and Annex table A3.2, see Background Paper 11 for details). Among nonagricultural occupations in both rural and urban areas (figure 3.2b), households with small businessmen and petty traders as the head had the highest relative per capita consumption, followed by higher-level employees (executives, officials, professionals, and teachers).

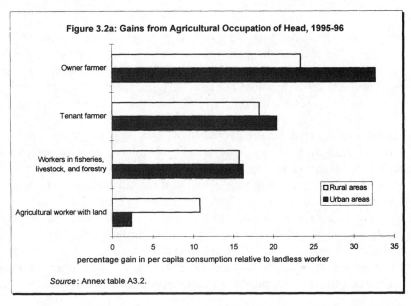

Figure 3.2a: Gains from Agricultural Occupation of Head, 1995-96

percentage gain in per capita consumption relative to landless worker

Source: Annex table A3.2.

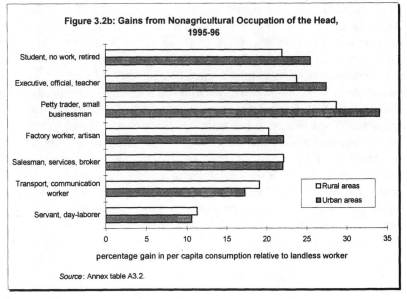

Figure 3.2b: Gains from Nonagricultural Occupation of the Head, 1995-96

percentage gain in per capita consumption relative to landless worker

Source: Annex table A3.2.

3.8   *The poorest agricultural households are likely to benefit the most from switching to the nonfarm sector.* Rural nonfarm households are almost always better off than rural landless agricultural households. Would poor rural landless households benefit from efforts to promote the rural nonfarm sector, say through access to credit and rural infrastructure? The potential difficulty with the answer to this question is that landless agricultural households tend to be not only poor, but also poorly endowed in characteristics (such as educational attainment) conducive to success in nonfarm activities. Our work shows, however, that controlling for observable household characteristics, the average expected gain in per capita consumption for a household head leaving the farm sector to join the nonfarm sector is about 6 percent of per capita consumption (Background Paper 2). And the gains tend to be the largest for the poorest farm households. For example, if a landless farm worker were to become a rural transportation worker, his household would enjoy a 16 percent increase in its per capita consumption. If this landless worker were to instead become a rural petty-trader, household per capita consumption would rise by 23 percent. Promoting the nonfarm sector will therefore enhance consumption and reduce poverty, specially of the poorest.

3.9   *Gains from nonfarm occupations vary greatly by region.* We have also found that there are large regional differences in the gains from switching to the nonfarm sector—nonfarm occupations appear to be more lucrative in the periphery of large urban centers, such as Dhaka. But, if the priority is poverty reduction, efforts to promote nonfarm activities should be directed at the poorest areas where the poorest households will benefit the most even if the average gains for the area may not be highest.

Landlessness increases the probability of being poor

3.10   *Consumption gains from owning land in rural areas are high.*   In addition to looking at consumption gains by occupation, we can also directly measure the per capita consumption gains associated with land ownership while controlling for other characteristics (Annex table A3.3). Average consumption gains for landholding are higher in rural than in urban areas, unless the landholding is less than half an acre. Consumption gains rise sharply as the size of the landholding increases. Compared to a landless rural household, a rural household with less than half an acre enjoyed 7 percent higher average household consumption, and a household with at least 2.5 acres enjoyed 43 percent higher per capita consumption in 1995-96. These consumption gains have been stable between 1988 and 1996 (the returns cannot be estimated for previous years because information on landholdings is not available in the HES.

3.11   Simulations of the effect on poverty incidence of taxing large landowners and transferring revenues to the landless and near landless (which can also be interpreted as implementing land redistribution under certain assumptions) suggest that these policies may be limited in their ability to reduce poverty (Ravallion and Sen 1994). Redistribution, in a country like Bangladesh where standards of living are low on average, may have a limited impact on poverty. Moreover, the impact of land redistribution on growth is uncertain. On the one hand, research has shown that smaller landowners tend to be more productive per unit of land than large landowners. There is also evidence that tenancy reform has promoted agricultural growth in West Bengal in India. On the other hand, land redistribution and a weakening of property rights may adversely affect investment, thereby reducing growth. While a more detailed analysis is required to establish the long-term consequences of land reform, some reallocation, or at least a fragmentation of landholdings, may already be taking place. According to the HES, the proportion of large landowners (more than 2.5 acres) in rural areas has fallen from 20 to 14 percent between 1988 and 1996, with a corresponding rise in the proportion of small landowners (0.05 to 1.49 acres). The proportion of the landless has remained stable.

Wage trends confirm the decline in poverty, and the slower decline in rural poverty

3.12 *Real wages have increased, but the agricultural wage has lagged behind other wages.* The consumption gains associated with different occupations provide us with a measure of the impact of occupation on household consumption at a point in time, but they do not tell us how real wages have evolved over time in various sectors. The national average real wage was 30 percent higher in 1996 than in 1983, (see figure 3.3 and Annex table A3.4) confirming the improvement

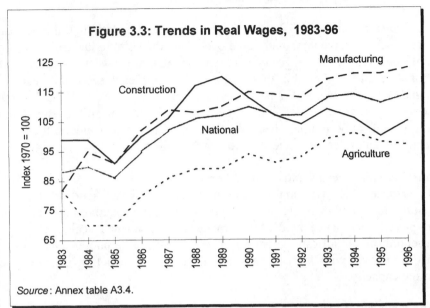

over the same period in living standards shown by the poverty measures in chapter 1. The trends in real wages differ by sector. Wages in agriculture have lagged behind wages in manufacturing and the general average wage. In manufacturing, the real wage was 50 percent higher in 1996 as compared to 1983. In contrast, real agricultural wages were only 18 percent higher in 1996 than in 1983. Furthermore, they did not keep up with inflation during the 1980s, confirming the stagnation in rural poverty incidence over the 1980s that was noted in chapter 1. The agricultural wage data used here are from the National Income Wing of the BBS. Alternative data from the Agricultural Statistics Wing (which are likely to be of better quality) suggest that agricultural wages have lagged behind manufacturing even further.

3.13 *Unemployment and underemployment are higher in rural areas.* In addition to smaller increases in their real wages, rural agricultural worker households suffer from higher unemployment and underemployment. According to the 1995-96 Labor Force Survey of the BBS, the unemployment rate—all people in the labor force who were unemployed or working less than 15 hours per week as a share of the labor force—was much higher in rural areas (17.6 percent) than in urban areas (11.3 percent) and than nationally (16.5 percent; figure 3.4). Similarly, the underemployment rate—people working less than 35 hours per week as a share of the working

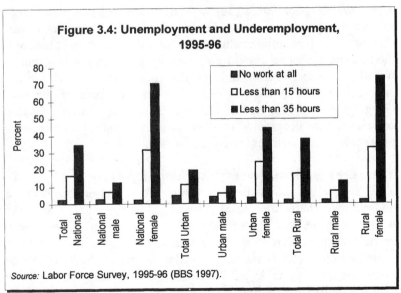

Note: Unemployment (no work or no work and work less than 15 hours) as share of labor force; underemployment (work less than 35 hours) as share of working population.

population—was higher in rural areas (37.9 percent) than in urban areas (19.6 percent) and than nationally (34.6 percent). In both urban and rural areas the unemployment and underemployment rates are higher for women than for men (Annex table A3.5).

3.14 *Unemployment rates are higher for the educated.* Although the per capita consumption gains from better education have remained stable over time, the better educated show higher unemployment rates. Of people over 15 years of age, unemployment rates are lowest for those with no education (0.7 percent nationally) and highest for those who have completed secondary education (10.3 percent) or have obtained a higher degree (9.2 percent; Annex table A3.6.) Part of this difference may be due to the higher reservation wage of better educated youth, who can afford to spend more time looking for better employment opportunities because their families can support them. Among the better-educated, unemployment rates are higher for women than for men.

Household size has an impact on poverty
3.15 Households with many children under 15 years tend to have lower levels of per capita consumption—and therefore to be poorer. Overall, the negative impact of household size on consumption and poverty incidence holds for a range of equivalence scales. But, if economies of scale within households are significant, larger households need not be poorer. Our results using 1995-96 data suggest that households with four or more adults tend to fare better, probably because of greater household earning capacity.

3.16 Changes in demographic characteristics—for example, a decrease in household size over time—and in the returns to those characteristics accounted for a relatively large share of the changes in per capita consumption between 1983 and 1996. For example, the number of adults in a household was found to have a greater impact in reducing poverty in recent years. Although more analysis is needed to understand the forces at work, this change may be the result of women's higher participation in labor markets and in self-employment (see Background Paper 11).

AREA CHARACTERISTICS

3.17 *Should poor areas be targeted?* Governmental and nongovernmental agencies often target resources to poor areas—aimed both at investing in the poor directly and at improving characteristics of poor areas such as infrastructure. If poverty depended on household characteristics alone, not on location, then public resources should go primarily to investing in these characteristics, such as education. We would still observe higher poverty incidence in some areas, but mainly because of the concentration of poor households in these areas, rather than because of the characteristics of the areas themselves. Geographic targeting would then have a rationale only if unobserved household characteristics were correlated with geography, or if the cost of targeting were lower if geographical variables rather than household characteristics were used for targeting.

There are significant geographic effects on poverty
3.18 Our work shows that poor areas are not poor just because they have a concentration of poor households. There are spatial differences in the returns to given household characteristics, such as education. Moreover, some spatial differences are independent of any obvious differences in observable household characteristics or differences in the returns to those characteristics (Background Paper 1). For example households living in the Dhaka district are better off than otherwise identical households living elsewhere (Annex table A3.7). Households in the districts of the Chittagong division (Chittagong, Comilla, Sylhet, and Noakhali) are also better off, especially those in rural areas.

3.19 *Geographic differences in poverty are largely explained by different area characteristics.* The relative importance of geographic effects can be measured by comparing actual headcount ratios with simulated headcount ratios for which suitable controls have been applied. Doing so will isolate the pure effects on living standards of geographic location on the one hand and household characteristics on the other. We computed two sets of conditional, simulated measures of poverty for 34 geographic locations (the 34 areas correspond to the rural and urban areas of 17 greater districts or combinations of districts) using the 1991-92 HES. One set, the "geographic profile," controls for household characteristics, so that the differences revealed can be attributed to geographic effects. The other set, the "concentration profile," controls for location, so that the differences can be attributed to household effects. In rural areas, for example, the observed headcount ratios vary by district from 11 to 65 percent (Annex table A3.7.) The headcount ratios obtained in the geographic profile are similar—they vary from 9 to 62 percent. By contrast, there is much less variation in the concentration profile, with rural headcount ratios ranging from 44 to 58 percent. This finding indicates that difference in area characteristics, rather than differences in household characteristics between areas, largely explain geographic differences in poverty. The results are similar for urban areas. They are also similar when using 1988-89 data, suggesting that the differences have been persistent. Further analysis is needed to identify which area characteristics account for these differences.

3.20 *Migration patterns correspond to the differences in area characteristics.* These differences in area characteristics should lead to migration, specially if the expected gains from moving are large. Bangladesh has relatively few (obvious) social, physical, or governmental impediments to internal migration. And, in fact, the geographic effects accord with independent evidence on rural-to-urban migration. The 1991 Census estimated that the number of annual, lifetime net migrants is positive for the Dhaka (and to a lesser extent Rajshahi) division, and negative for the Barisal, Chittagong, and Khulna divisions. This result should not be surprising given that an observationally equivalent household is less poor in the Dhaka Standard Metropolitan Area than elsewhere.

3.21 We can use a simple decomposition to measure the impact of changes in the gains from living in specific areas on per capita consumption over time (Background Paper 11). The decomposition indicates that the differential in living standards between the capital district of Dhaka and all other areas widened considerably over 1983-91, and then did not change much over 1992-96. With few constraints on migration, the rural to urban population shifts observed in recent years can be expected to continue unless significant investments are made to enhance the welfare of poorer rural areas.

3.22 *Improving area characteristic will reduce poverty.* The strong effects of geography on household consumption indicates that investments designed to improve area characteristics should play an important role in poverty reduction, especially in rural areas. Thus, the government's policy of concentrating rural investments on selected growth centers should be complemented by public, NGO, and private investments targeted to the poorest areas.

DETERMINANTS OF INEQUALITY

3.23 *Education, landownership and location are the main determinants of inequality.* The microeconomic determinants of per capita consumption and poverty discussed so far also affect inequality. Secondary education of a household spouse raises her household's average consumption, but it also increases inequality relative to other (poorer) households. Here, we estimate conditional measures of between-group inequality (see Background Paper 11). These measure the impact of individual area and selected household characteristics on inequality, controlling for other characteristics. The higher is the conditional, between-group inequality associated with location or a characteristic, the more it contributes to the total inequality in per capita consumption, measured by the overall Gini coefficient (Annex table

A3.8). Education of the household head contributes the most to inequality in urban areas, in large part because the returns to education for household heads who have completed secondary school are high. This contribution has been rising. Education of the spouse contributes less to total inequality in rural areas as compared to urban areas: in rural areas it also contributes the least to inequality as compared to the other characteristics. Land ownership drives inequality more than any other household attribute in rural areas. Location is the second largest determinant of inequality in both urban and rural areas. Occupation has a smaller impact on inequality, and this impact has decreased over time.

3.24   Do these determinants of inequality pose a policy tradeoff? Not necessarily. For example, while public spending for universities may increase inequality, funding for primary school reduces both poverty and inequality. Enabling the poor to complete primary school or enhance their skills through programs such as Food for Education and Vulnerable Group Development would help to reduce inequality. The same situation holds for household land ownership in rural areas: enabling the landless to own some land would be both poverty and inequality reducing even though land is a key determinant of inequality overall. Investments in poorer areas that improve area characteristics would help to reduce geography's contribution to inequality. If there is a trade-off between reducing poverty and increasing inequality the reduction of poverty should have priority in Bangladesh.

SUMMARY

3.25   In Bangladesh, as in many other countries, household characteristics are related to poverty:
- Education is the key determinant of urban living standards, and to a lesser extent also of rural living standards.
- Land ownership is the key determinant of the rural living standards.
- The returns to education are similar for household heads and spouses.
- The returns to education and to land have remained relatively stable over time.
- There are large differences in standards of living by occupation

The percentage gains in per capita consumption associated with these household characteristics can guide policy design and cost-benefit evaluations.

3.26   If poverty depended on household characteristics alone and not on area characteristics, there would be little incentive for targeting investments to relatively poorer areas. Differences in poverty between regions:
- Depend more on area characteristics than on differences in the characteristics of the households living in those areas.
- Provide a strong justification for targeting investment to poor areas.

3.27   The next step would be to explain what determines area effects on living standards by attempting to answer questions such as: Does the density of the road network matter more than electrification? Do household characteristics (such as education levels) matter for regional development, suggesting the existence of positive externalities? Are geographic differences in living standards a result of differences in social capital? These are difficult questions to be sure. But, it may be possible to answer them in future using panel data techniques similar to those illustrated in chapter 2.

3.28   Ninety three percent of the very poor live in rural areas, where nonagricultural households are better off on average than landless farm households. Our results suggest that:
- The gains from switching from the farm to nonfarm sector are positive on average for farm households as a whole, and are the largest for the poorest farm households.
- There is a strong justification for microcredit and other policies that expand rural occupational choice.

3.29   Some household characteristics associated with lower poverty also contribute to inequality. These results suggest that enabling the poor, particularly girls, to complete primary school, for example through programs such as Food for Education (discussed in chapter 4) and investments in poorer areas that improve area characteristics, would help to reduce inequality.

OVERVIEW OF CHAPTER 4. PUBLIC EXPENDITURES AND GOVERNMENT PROGRAMS

PARA.	KEY CONCLUSIONS	POLICY IMPLICATIONS
4.2 to 4.3	**Social sector expenditures** Since 1990, the share of the Annual Development Program (ADP) devoted to the social sector has more than doubled. In future years spending for education and health will continue to rise, reaching 30 percent of ADP spending. This is higher than other South Asian countries.	The increase in social spending has contributed to progress in the social sectors. While the focus on health and education is appropriate for promoting human development of the poor, the increase in social spending must address concerns about quality and sustainability and must be well-targeted. Broader public sector governance issues must be addressed in improving service delivery.
4.4 to 4.10	**Public expenditures on health** Health care improves not only well being, but also earning capacity. Per capita costs for medical treatment remain high. Although in rural areas public spending on health is devoted about equally to the nonpoor and the poor (the bottom half of the rural population absorbed 57 percent of public expenditures on health), there remains considerable scope for better targeting public health expenditures.	There is a strong case for public provisioning of basic health care to the poor, but quality and targeting must improve. Given budget constraints, the focus should be on a package of basic services, reproductive health care, child health services, communicable disease control, and promotion of behavioral changes. These have positive externalities and are less likely to be offered by private providers.
4.11 to 4.16	**Public expenditures on education** Despite progress, attendance remains low in primary and secondary schools. Drop-outs and repeats are frequent. Attending primary school does not ensure literacy. The bottom half of the rural population benefits from only 38 percent of rural public education expenditures. Education spending benefits the rich more than the poor because the poor do not participate as often at secondary and higher levels.	Education reduces poverty, and public expenditures must therefore improve coverage, quality, and efficiency of schooling for the poor. Investments in education should continue to receive high priority. The priority for public funding should be given to primary and secondary education. Gender equity should be pursued in secondary school (through the stipend program) and possibly at higher levels.
4.17 to 4.19	**Safety nets** Food safety nets are an essential component of the government's strategy to fight poverty. Food for Work provides relief in rural areas in slack seasons while helping to maintain rural infrastructure. Vulnerable Group Development contributes to the empowerment and earning potential of poor women. Vulnerable Group Development includes an investment component, and participating women benefit from skill, literacy, and numeracy training; access to microcredit; and health and nutrition education. Food for Education promotes primary school enrollment. Food for Education holds the promise of high social returns and equity gains in the future. Though their benefits are difficult to compare, all three appear to be cost-effective, with Food for Work and Vulnerable Group Development better targeted.	Safety nets in Bangladesh offer both transfer payments and the opportunity for human capital accumulation. To increase the welfare impact of these food-based programs, as well as their efficiency and coverage, monetization options should be explored, as should better means of targeting.
4.20 to 4.29	**Food for Education program** Food for Education is the fastest growing food distribution program. It accounts for 43 percent of the primary education budget in the 1997-98 ADP. Food for Education increases primary school attendance for poor children by 21 percent and has been found to be cost-effective in its program impact despite imperfect targeting.	Although Food for Education raises enrollment and attendance, it does not increase school quality—a major concern. Improving the quality and efficiency of primary education (to complete the cycle in a shorter period) would increase the cost effectiveness of Food for Education, as would better targeting. The needs of Food for Education must be balanced against the overall needs of primary education.

CHAPTER 4: PUBLIC EXPENDITURES AND GOVERNMENT SAFETY NET PROGRAMS

4.1   Effective public spending, including spending on rural and urban infrastructure in addition to social sector programs and safety nets, can reduce poverty. This chapter focuses on health, education, and safety net programs because they are among the fastest growing public expenditures in Bangladesh. In 1989-90 social expenditures made up 10 percent of total Annual Development Program (ADP) outlays. By 2001, according to the Fifth Five-Year Plan, ADP expenditures on social sectors will amount to 30 percent of total ADP spending (more than Tk 63 billion). Most of this rise will finance education and health, two sectors that are important for the poor. But how much will the poor benefit? The next section addresses this question.

4.2   Public safety net programs can also protect the poor. Do these programs attain their objectives? Are they well-targeted? The second section deals with safety nets, focusing on Food for Education, a rapidly growing program that is designed to boost primary school enrollment and attendance among poor children. Underlying the public expenditure focus of this chapter are fundamental issues of governance, institutional arrangements, and the role of public, NGO, and private agencies. Though we do not deal explicitly with these issues, it is clear that outcomes for the poor are closely related to the quality, accessibility, and sustainability of public services.[1]

PUBLIC EXPENDITURES

4.3   *Public social sector expenditures are rising rapidly.* Social spending in real terms rose from less than Tk 8 billion in 1989-90 to Tk 28.5 billion in 1995-96 in constant 1995-96 prices (figure 4.1a, Annex table A4.1). Real education spending has increased the most, both in absolute and relative terms, from Tk 3.15 billion in 1989-90 to Tk 15.88 billion in 1995-96. Public health spending has also increased dramatically, from Tk 1.37 billion in 1989-90 to Tk 5.85 billion in 1995-96. Education and health together represented 80 percent of ADP social spending in 1995-96; the other outlays are devoted to family planning and social welfare. Overall, the share of Bangladesh's ADP devoted to education, health, social welfare, and family planning has more than doubled since 1989-90, from 10 to 24 percent (figure 4.1b).

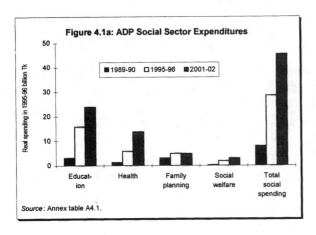

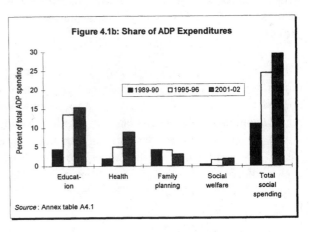

---

[1] For recent reviews of public expenditures see World Bank (1996d and 1997c). For discussions of public expenditures in specific sectors see World Bank (1996b) on rural infrastructure; World Bank (1996a) on education; Government of Bangladesh (1997) on health and population; and World Bank (1997d) on municipal expenditures.

4.4   In future years spending for education and health will continue to rise in real terms. According to the Fifth Five-Year Plan, by 2000-01 real spending for education will increase by another 50 percent, reaching Tk 23.88 billion (in 1995-96 taka); spending for health will more than double, reaching Tk 13.8 billion; and overall social spending will represent close to 30 percent of ADP outlays. These planned increases are likely to outpace planned social spending increases in other South Asian countries. But how much will the poor share in the benefits of this rapidly increasing social spending?

The case for public provision of basic health care to the poor is strong, but quality must improve
4.5   Good health has a direct, positive impact on the quality of life. It contributes to a person's capabilities and raises earnings capacity. Research by Haider and others (1997) using the 1994-95 Health and Demographic Survey indicates that 41 percent of rural people who were sick and 32 percent of urban people who were sick lost an average of 20 days of work per person. Annual per capita treatment costs were relatively high, at about Tk 900 in urban areas and Tk 600 in rural areas. In both urban and rural areas this amount is equal to or higher than the regional monthly poverty lines. Access to affordable health care for the poor is therefore vital. It is also important that the poor be able to take advantage of higher quality health services: too often the gains from improved quality are captured by the nonpoor, even those in basic services (for a discussion of the relationships between public spending on health and health outcomes, see Filmer and Pritchett 1997).

4.6   *Bangladesh has made substantial progress in health and family planning.* Fertility has decreased, in part due to the rising use of contraceptives (Cleland and others 1994). Child immunization has reached 70 percent. Life expectancy rose from 45 years in 1970 to 58 years in 1996. From 1981 to 1992 the population-to-doctor ratio fell by half, to 5,242, and the population-to-nurse ratio declined by two-thirds, to 5,709. The number of hospitals has increased more slowly, but has kept pace with population growth so that the population-to-bed ratio has remained stable.

4.7   *Major health challenges remain.* Maternal and infant mortality rates are very high by international standards. Many children are malnourished, with numbers higher in rural than in urban areas. Less than 40 percent of the population has access to basic health services. And due in part to lower contraceptive use by less-educated women, fertility rates remain one-third higher for rural illiterate women than for women who have completed primary school (Mabud, Hossain, and Haque 1997). The longer-term challenges are daunting: over the next 30 years Bangladesh's population (124 million) will increase by 60 million people due to the momentum created by several decades of rapid demographic growth.

4.8   The Health and Population Sector Strategy, prepared by the government and donors in 1997, recommends focusing on an essential package of basic services. Current government health expenditures are estimated to be $2.7 per capita per year, while the cost of an essential package of services recommended by the Health and Population Sector Strategy is estimated at $4.1 per capita per year. Given budget constraints, prioritizing expenditures is essential. The Strategy recommends that the focus should be on reproductive health, maternal and child health, communicable diseases, simple curative care, and social communication to promote behavioral change. Health services in these areas have proven externalities, and private health services providers are less likely to offer them. Partnerships with Bangladesh's NGOs and greater community participation will help the government reach its objectives. For example, the success of the government's pilot Integrated Nutrition Project is closely related to its field implementation by NGOs and community participation in nutrition activities. This project is expected to be replicated nationwide to address Bangladesh's massive malnutrition problem.

4.9   *Rural public health expenditures should be better targeted.* The focus of the Health and Population Sector Strategy on basic services is appropriate in the context of poverty reduction. Evidence compiled by the Center for Integrated Rural Development for Asia and Pacific in Dhaka (CIRDAP 1997b) suggests that in rural areas public health expenditures are equally divided between the nonpoor and the poor, rather than predominantly devoted to the nonpoor: for example, the bottom half of the rural population benefited from 57 percent of public expenditures on health (figure 4.2, Annex table A4.2). The correlation between income decile and share of public health spending is close to zero. Although one could argue that such evenly distributed

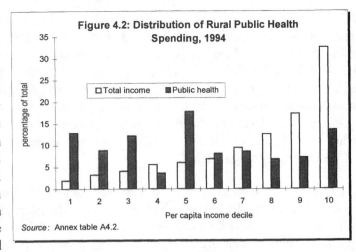

Figure 4.2: Distribution of Rural Public Health Spending, 1994

Source: Annex table A4.2.

rural public expenditures for health reduce inequality (they are akin to a flat transfer payment to all), there clearly remains considerable scope for better targeting, (see World Bank 1996d).

4.10   Focusing on public expenditures alone is misleading when there are weak links between public spending and actual improvements in health status because of poor service quality. This is the case in Bangladesh. Filmer, Hammer, and Pritchett (1998) argue that there are some basic services for which market failures are less severe and thus could be provided efficiently by the private sector. But because the very poor who cannot afford private basic health services are so numerous in Bangladesh, the equity case for public provision and subsidy of basic health services to the poor is strong.

The case for public expenditures on education for the poor is strong, but quality and access must improve

4.11   The government has recognized the role of education in promoting growth and reducing poverty. As a result, the country has made substantial progress. School enrollment has increased dramatically, almost doubling in percentage terms in the 1980s according to data from the 1981 and 1991 censuses. But, while 8 of 10 children aged 5 to 11 currently enroll in school, attendance rates are as low as 60 percent (some students attend non-formal schools, which are not reflected in the official data, hence actual attendance and enrollment rates are higher than these figures). Dropout rates are high, since only 6 of 10 students complete primary school. Among those completing primary education, repeats are frequent. It takes on average nearly 9 years for a student to complete the 5 years of primary school. Dropout rates for secondary school are even higher, with only one-third of students completing their studies. It takes nearly 13 years on average to complete the 5 years of secondary school.

4.12   *Quality of education remains a major issue.* Attending primary school does not ensure literacy. Greaney, Khandker, and Alam (1997) show that one-third of rural school-going children aged 11 or higher do not meet standard, minimum levels of performance in reading, writing, written mathematics, and oral mathematics. Acknowledging the low quality of education, the Bank's 1996 Education Expenditure Review recommended shifting the focus from expanding enrollment to improving the quality and efficiency of schooling (World Bank 1996a). Doing so by providing better pay and training to teachers will cost money, but it will also save money. In government primary schools, the cost per graduate in 1993-94 was Tk 6,403. This figure would drop to Tk 3,680 if the cycle was completed in five years. For secondary schools, the potential savings are even larger—the current average expenditure per graduate of Tk 28,174 would drop to Tk 16,994 if the cycle were completed on time. The savings for university students would amount to an even larger share of university education spending.

4.13   *Increasing girl's education should be a priority.* Chapter 3 suggested that the gains in per capita consumption if the spouse of a household head was educated are as large or larger than the gains from better-educated household heads. Raising the educational attainment of women should therefore be the highest priority, since it also provides public externalities, for example, reduced maternal and child mortality and better control of communicable diseases (Summers 1994). While progress has been made toward gender equity, girls remain underrepresented at all levels of schooling. In 1993-94 girls represented 43 percent of all primary school students, 41 percent of secondary students, 31 percent of higher secondary students, 23 percent of university students, and only 5 percent of technical education and vocational training students.

4.14   Programs such as Food for Education (discussed below) and secondary school stipends for girls can help boost school enrollment and attendance. Khandker (1996) shows that better-educated mothers are more likely to send their children to school. Using HES data we show that parents' education has a significant impact on children's enrollment and attendance (Background Paper 3). Since adult literacy in rural areas according to the 1991 Census was only 39 percent for men and 21 percent for women, adult education programs should be effective in raising children's school attendance, in addition to increasing the earning potential of adults.

4.15   Both household and community variables affect school attendance. The higher is the proportion of children in a household, the lower is the household's mean attendance rate, possibly because of crowding out effects (see Background Paper 3). If the main school in a village is a private school, primary school attendance is significantly higher. Villages in which parents complain about the lack of secondary institutions for girls or the poor quality of teachers have a significantly lower number of children in primary school. As with health services, it is important that the poor gain from higher quality as well as broader coverage. Given that government services suffer from quality problems NGOs should play a major role in helping to improve service standards and ensuring that the services are targeted to the poor.

4.16   *Public expenditures on education need to be more pro-poor.* Data for 1994 (CIRDAP 1997a) indicate that the poorest decile of the rural population receives only 6.9 percent of rural public expenditures on education (figure 4.3, Annex table A4.3). Overall, the bottom half of the population receives only 38.4 percent of education expenditures. By contrast, the top decile receives 15.4 percent. Primary education expenditures are more evenly distributed with the poorest decile receiving 9.5 percent. But secondary and higher education expenditures are not, with the poorest decile receiving 3.0 percent of secondary education spending and 0.8 percent of higher education spending. Given the strong effect of education on consumption and poverty, public expenditures on education should clearly be made more pro-poor (World Bank 1996d, 1997c). This could be achieved by increasing the poor's attendance in primary and secondary school and letting the private sector pick up a greater share of spending for higher education.

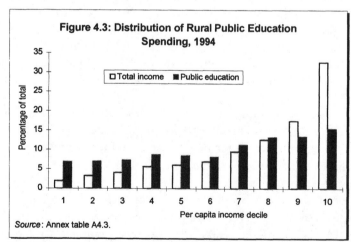

Figure 4.3: Distribution of Rural Public Education Spending, 1994

☐ Total income   ■ Public education

Percentage of total

Per capita income decile

Source: Annex table A4.3.

GOVERNMENT SAFETY NET PROGRAMS

4.17   Safety nets in Bangladesh serve both transfer payment and human capital accumulation objectives. There is a long tradition of safety nets funded by external food aid. The three biggest programs are Food for Work, which provides wheat in exchange for work in rural infrastructure projects, Food for Education which initially provided wheat and now provides wheat and rice to poor children in return for regular primary school attendance, and Vulnerable Group Development, which provides food grain and training to disadvantaged women. Test Relief is a smaller program used to support activities like cleaning ponds and bushes, and making minor repairs to rural roads, schools, mosques, and madrasahs during the rainy season.

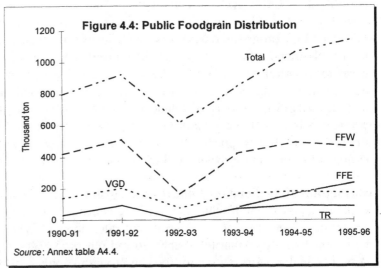

Source: Annex table A4.4.

Note: FFW is Food for Work, VGD is Vulnerable Group Development, FFE is Food for Education, TR is Test Relief.

Food for Work is by far the largest program, but the fastest growing (and second largest) program is Food for Education, which was started in 1993-94 in selected rural villages (see figure 4.4 and Annex table A4.4).

The Costs of transferring one taka to the poor is roughly similar across programs, except Food for Work

4.18   The unit transfer costs of the various food-based safety net programs are similar in size. Ahmed and Billah (1994; see also Subbarao and others 1997) estimate these costs taking into account administrative costs and leakage to the nonpoor. The cost of transferring 1 taka in benefits to the poor through these programs was Tk 1.59 for Food for Education, Tk 1.56 for Vulnerable Group Development, and Tk 2.06 for Food for Work (under World Food Program management). The lowest cost is that of the Rural Maintenance Program, which employs destitute women in a labor-intensive rural road maintenance work (Tk 1.32). Food for Work, Vulnerable Group Development, and Test Relief are generally well targeted to the poor, so that leakage does not contribute much to the overall cost (figure 4.5, Annex table A4.5). Leakage appears to be higher for Food

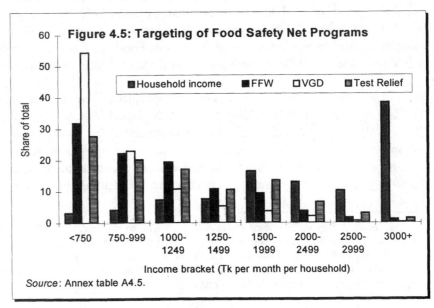

Source: Annex table A4.5.

for Education (see discussion below). When compared to public works programs in other countries, Bangladesh's programs appear to be performing well in terms of cost effectiveness. However, the efficiency of the programs could be improved. Dorosh and Haggblade (1995) suggest that monetization would increase benefits by 16 percent thanks to the savings in commodity handling costs, especially in the case of Food for Work.

4.19   Which programs should be given priority? The benefits of the various programs extend beyond the simple transfer payment and are therefore difficult to compare. Food for Work provides immediate relief to the rural poor and helps build and maintain rural infrastructure, which is important for rural development. Vulnerable Group Development was originally a pure transfer program, but it now also includes a skill-investment component—NGOs working in partnership with the government, provide women with skill, literacy, and numeric training; credit; and health and nutrition education. Food for Education, by raising primary school attendance, offers high future returns, not only for the children themselves, but also for society as a whole.

Evaluation of the Food for Education program

4.20   Given the high returns to primary education in many countries, it should be no surprise that programs designed to increase enrollment rates abound. What is surprising is that these programs have not been frequently evaluated. Subbarao and others (1997) report that of 97 programs surveyed in Latin America, including many school feeding programs, only ten had been evaluated (apparently only three evaluated well). Most evaluations focus only on coverage, few measure program impacts, and fewer still assess cost effectiveness.

4.21   Many poor households may not send their children to school because they cannot afford direct schooling costs and/or the opportunity costs of the children's help in the home or outside the home. Food for Education was launched in 1993 to address this situation. Its objectives are to increase enrollment and attendance rates and reduce dropout rates. Participating children receive monthly rations of wheat or rice (wheat from food-aid was used in the early years) if they attend at least 85 percent of their primary school classes. Food for Education has grown rapidly. It is expected to cost Tk 3.4 billion in fiscal 1998, accounting for 43 percent of ADP's primary education budget.

4.22   To participate in Food for Education, schools and children must pass through a two-step selection procedure. First, economically backward administrative units at the union level are selected. Within these unions, Food for Education support is granted to most schools, whether government-run or not. Second, within schools, poor children are targeted by household land ownership (landless or near landless households), parents' occupations (day laborers and poorly paid artisans), and family structure (female household heads). Households benefiting from Food for Education cannot also receive assistance from the Vulnerable Group Development and Rural Maintenance programs.

4.23   *Previous evaluations have shown mixed results.* The International Food Policy Research Institute (IFPRI; Ahmed and Billah 1994) and the Bangladesh Institute for Development Studies (BIDS 1997) have evaluated the Food for Education program. These evaluations were based on before-and-after comparisons of mean outcomes of a treatment group (beneficiary schools) and a control group (nonbeneficiary schools). Treatment and control group methods are valid only if schools have been *randomly* assigned to treatment and control groups.[2] But placement has not been randomized. This could

---

2   The issue of program placement can be illustrated with an example. Consider two schools. The first, which is better than the second, grows at a rate of 10 percent in year 1, while the second grows at 5 percent. Without Food for Education, in year 2 the growth rates of the two schools would have been 10 percent and 2 percent. With Food for Education granted to the second school, its growth rate in year 2 is maintained at 5 percent. If one does not take into account the fact that the second school was targeted by the program precisely because of its difficulties, a simple comparison of the outcomes for the two schools would not

explain why the evaluations by IFPRI and BIDS are contradictory to some extent: IFPRI found a statistically significant positive enrollment gain for girls (31 percent) and boys (27 percent). But BIDS' work, literally interpreted, suggests that Food for Education had a negative impact on enrollment, that is the introduction of Food for Education reduced enrollment growth in participating schools.

4.24   *Food for Education is cost-effective in terms of its program impact.* Data from the 1995-96 HES and an appropriate econometric model to control for the endogeniety of program placement at the individual level   show that Food for Education does raise enrollment and attendance rates (see Background Paper 3). Enrollment and attendance of all primary-school-age children in the household increased by 21.1 percent for every 100 kg of foodgrain per year that the participating household received. Since there are on average 2.1 such children in each household (or older children who have not yet completed primary school), this result implies that sending the equivalent of one more child to primary school full time for one year would take 226 kg of foodgrain (i.e. 100/(.211 x 2.1)).

4.25   Food for Education suffers from program leakages and is less well targeted than other food safety net programs. One-third of its beneficiaries come from households with per capita consumption above the upper poverty lines. As a result of this targeting leakage, it would take 332 kg of foodgrain per year to put one more *poor* child in primary school full time. Half the beneficiaries come from households with average consumption levels above the lower poverty lines. It would therefore take 475 kg of foodgrain to put one more *very poor* child in school full time (see Background Paper 10).

4.26   How cost effective is Food for Education? We answer this question by estimating how much a participant's per capita consumption rises in the future as a result of having completed primary school. This is a fundamentally different (and more appropriate in the context of program impact) evaluation of Food for Education than simply adding up current program costs and comparing them to the current value of the foodgrain transferred. We estimate that the annual cost of one more poor child attending primary school through Food for Education is $66.4, while the cost of having one more very poor child attend primary school is $95. These costs take into account not only the cost of the grain, but also the cost of its transport and delivery and the leakage to the nonpoor. These costs are higher than those estimated by Summers (1994) for India ($32) and Kenya ($58), in large part because we have taken the leakage to the nonpoor into account. The additional per capita consumption enjoyed by the child and his or her family when the child reaches adulthood is $52.6 per year for the very poor and $69.9 for the poor, not taking into account the direct benefit of the food received. (Including the value of the direct consumption of foodgrain, or its sale and use for other purposes would improve cost-effectiveness. Similarly, including the opportunity cost to the household of the child going to school would reduce cost-effectiveness.) Since the average student completes the 5 years of primary school over a much longer period of time, we assume that the young adult starts earning only at age 20, and further assume that the benefits provided by a better education last for 38 years. With these assumptions and the resulting stream of benefits, the discount rate needed to break even was estimated at 3.61 percent for the very poor, and 5.84 percent for the poor (the greater the stream of future benefits the higher the discount rate, and the more cost-effective the program).

4.27   These discount rates measure the private returns to education, but do yet account for the direct consumption benefits from the foodgrain received. If we also include the value of foodgrain consumed, or its sale and use for other purposes, the discount rates would rise. Administrative and delivery costs represent one-third of the program costs and foodgrain itself represents the other two-thirds. Including the

reveal any impact of Food for Education because the counterfactual of a 2 percent growth rate would not be recognized. Appropriate econometric techniques can help in highlighting such counterfactuals, while simple before-and- after comparisons of outcomes cannot.

value of foodgrain received would lower the net costs of enabling one poor or very poor child to attend school full time by two-thirds, in which case the private rates of return would increase to 8.11 for the very poor, and 11.50 for the poor. To estimate the social returns, we need to add the value of externalities to these private returns. As noted by Summers (1994) for India and Kenya, the positive externalities—for example the future public savings in health, family planning, and nutrition costs achieved through better education for girls—tend to be large. Adding such positive externalities to the already high private rates of return would yield social rates of return that would, under most circumstances, be substantially greater than the social cost of funds, making Food for Education cost effective in terms of its program impact.

The Food for Education program should be improved

4.28   Even if Food for Education is cost-effective, its performance could be improved. If school efficiency was increased by reducing the number of repeats by two-thirds, so that children would complete primary school in six years instead of almost nine, the discount rates for the very poor and the poor would rise. Alternatively, if targeting was improved by reducing leakage by two-thirds, the discount rates for the very poor and the poor rise even more. These figures seem to suggest that the gains for Food for Education from improving targeting would be larger than the gains from improving school efficiency. But of course, from a broader point of view, all children would benefit from better school efficiency, while only a portion of poor and very poor children would benefit from better targeting of Food for Education. The above simulations should therefore not be interpreted as an argument against improving school efficiency; they simply make the case for better targeting. Note that it would be useful to think about including incentives within Food for Education to help beneficiary children finish school faster, which could have spill-over effects for children not in the Food for Education program. But further research would be needed to ensure that such incentives do not work to the detriment of the poorest children, who may also be the ones who have the hardest time avoiding repeats. If Food for Education can be organized as a cash stipend program rather than as a food-based one, it is very likely that administrative costs would decline, thus further improving its cost-effectiveness.

4.29   Despite imperfect targeting, Food for Education seems to be cost-effective. But this by itself does not imply that the program should be pursued. Given the already large and growing education budget allocations to Food for Education, its growth clearly has substantial opportunity costs, especially since the program does not, by itself, improve the quality of primary schools—still a major issue. Moreover, other targeted programs may be more cost-effective than Food for Education, but it is not clear what these other programs would be. Using 1991-92 data (before the start of Food for Education), Khandker (1996) found that reducing the cost of schooling (books, uniforms, school supplies) by 50 percent increased attendance for boys and girls by only 6 and 3 percent, respectively—much less than the 21.1 percent increase obtained with Food for Education. Food for Education also appears to be cheaper than school lunch programs. Thus, the above results would suggest that the government should continue to improve Food for Education given the need to reach the poor and hence the major role Food for Education is likely to play in primary education for some time. The government should also be mindful of the opportunity cost of Food for Education investments in human capital in terms of the additional investments in classrooms, teaching materials, and teachers.

SUMMARY

4.30   Social expenditures in the Annual Development Program will continue to rise, particularly in education and health. The evidence suggests that:
  ▪   Although the incidence of rural public spending on health is evenly distributed in the population and therefore somewhat redistributive (the poor benefit as much as others despite their lower

incomes) the targeting and quality of public health expenditures should be improved to benefit the poor more.

- To increase the impact that public spending on health has on poverty, priority should be given to providing a basic package of services including reproductive health, maternal and child health, communicable disease control, and simple curative care.
- Public spending on education remains biased toward the well-off. Reallocating public education expenditures toward primary and secondary schooling would help to increase the benefits for the poor.
- The quality and efficiency of education must increase to ensure that primary school enrollments translate into literacy. Reducing repetition rates in primary, secondary, and higher education would reduce the cost of public education, thereby freeing up resources to encourage school enrollment and attendance among the poor.
- The Food for Education program raises primary school enrollment and attendance and is cost-effective, but must be better targeted.

4.31   Public safety net programs such as Food for Work, Vulnerable Group Development, Test Relief, and Rural Maintenance play an important role in protecting the poor and in building rural infrastructure and human capital. Given the persistence of high poverty rates and the observed increases in inequality, these programs must be pursued. Monetization could bring additional benefits by reducing costs and avoiding risks of distortions in food markets.

OVERVIEW OF CHAPTER 5. NGO PROGRAMS

PARA.	KEY CONCLUSIONS	POLICY IMPLICATIONS
5.2 to 5.5	**NGOs in partnership with the government** Bangladesh is a pioneer in establishing innovative NGOs. Unlike most countries in which the government largely bears responsibility for overall development and NGOs focus on small projects, in Bangladesh several NGOs have reached a size that puts their poverty reduction programs on par with government programs.	The poor and variable quality of public services, particularly in the social sectors, and the proven grassroots record of many NGOs suggest a natural partnership between public and NGO programs. Such partnerships are increasing in number and should be promoted further.
5.6 to 5.8	**Microcredit programs** Microcredit programs are effective in fighting poverty. Research suggests that microcredit institutions such as Grameen Bank are becoming more sustainable over time because of their system of group-based collateral and high repayment rates. Yet it is unlikely that microcredit alone can be the solution to poverty reduction. Microcredit may not reach the poorest, and it may exclude small landowning entrepreneurs who are not eligible for microcredit but also do not have access to formal commercial credit.	With rapid growth in lending, it will be important to ensure that quantitative objectives (reaching as many households as possible) are not pursued at the cost of qualitative objectives (reaching the households that most need assistance). The government and microcredit providers must find ways, possibly through innovative partnerships, to reach the poorest, as well as borrowers who are ineligible for microcredit but do not have access to formal credit.
5.9 to 5.12	**Health care and education facilities** In rural areas NGOs provide health and education services that are of higher quality than government services and less expensive than private services. Complaints about government services suggest that the primary need in health care is to improve the quality rather than the quantity of public services. But, in education there are more complaints about the number of education facilities than about the quality of teachers. There, both quantity and quality concerns should continue to receive attention.	NGO rural health and education facilities suffer the least from complaints by users. The biggest complaint against NGO facilities was that they were too far, suggesting that more and nearer facilities would be highly welcome. The complaints against public services point to the areas of improvement that are likely to benefit users the most. The top two complaints against public institutions are poor service quality and lack of medicines for health and not enough primary and post primary schools for education. The vastly superior performance of NGO rural health and education services suggests clear possibilities for partnerships among NGOs, the government, and the private sector in providing better health and education services.
5.13 to 5.17	**Targeting the poor** Landownership is the primary targeting indicator for NGO and other programs. While this has many advantages, targeting efficiency can be improved by using other information, particularly in the context of reaching the poorest. While well targeted at the household level, NGO and public programs do not appear to be well targeted at the village level.	Land holding is a good targeting indicator for households, but targeting the landless in microcredit programs may not be enough to reach the poorest because they lack the skills to participate in group lending. Improved village-level targeting by both NGO and public programs may help to reach poorer households.

CHAPTER 5: NGO PROGRAMS

5.1   Bangladesh's NGOs are world renowned. The Grameen Bank, BRAC, Proshika, and the Association for Social Advancement (ASA) are among the largest rural development organizations in the country. The next section reviews the growth of NGOs and assesses their performance relative to that of the government in providing microcredit, health, and education services in rural areas. The last section examines how well microfinance programs target the poor.

NGOS AND SERVICE DELIVERY

5.2   *Bangladesh's NGOs are unique in their mandate, size, and orientation.* The traditional roles of NGOs and the government have become blurred in Bangladesh. In most countries NGOs tend to be small, focusing on project-specific issues of local interest, targeting interventions to specific local groups, promoting innovation, and advocating and initiating change. The government's activities tend to be larger in size and coverage, and usually have a much greater impact on overall development. But NGOs in Bangladesh go well beyond the traditional NGO strengths. Several of the large NGOs offer services that are superior in quality to public services and, taken together, larger in coverage.

5.3   The Grameen Bank had 2.06 million microcredit clients in 1996, mostly women, and BRAC, Proshika, and ASA had 1.84, 1.30, and 0.57 million, respectively. This puts the size of these organizations on par with the Bangladesh Rural Development Board (BRDB), the government's microcredit agency. In addition to microcredit, NGOs provide skill training, education, health and family planning services, and water supply and sanitation services. NGOs are also active in managing common property resources, extending nontraditional agriculture, and initiating income-generation activities. For these activities as well, some NGO programs have reached the size of similar government programs. BRAC's Non-Formal Primary Education program operated 34,175 schools in 1996, enrolling 1.1 million students in 22,602 villages. By comparison, the Food for Education program served about 2 million children that year. NGOs have also diversified their activities: BRAC acts as a rural financial intermediary providing microcredit to landless women nationwide and, for example, also supports research on plant tissue culture to improve agribusiness opportunities in fruit and vegetable cultivation. Grameen not only operates the Grameen Bank but has also sponsored Grameen Telecomm, which provides cellular telephone services.

5.4   This remarkable growth is not limited to large, internationally known NGOs. Some 20,000 NGOs have registered to date with the Department of Social Welfare: of these, many that are still active remain small. The NGO Affairs Bureau started registering foreign-funded NGOs in 1990: 1,185 such NGOs had registered by November 1997, most of them local. This number is rising (figure 5.1, Annex table A5.1.) The NGO Bureau also tracks information on foreign-funded NGO projects (figure 5.2, Annex table A5.2).

5.5   *NGO-government partnerships have increased.* The relationship between the government and NGOs has not always been smooth (World Bank 1996c). The government has been concerned about NGOs' cost-effectiveness, accountability, and heavy reliance on foreign funds. The NGOs, in turn, have criticized the government for being rigid and bureaucratic, for wanting to control rather than support NGOs, and for failing to differentiate among NGOs according to their performance. Many of these wrinkles have been ironed out in recent years, leading to a rapid rise in partnerships between the government, NGOs, and externally-funded projects in which NGOs are the executing agencies in the field. We discuss below two of the many areas NGOs are active in: microcredit and the provision of health and education services in rural areas.

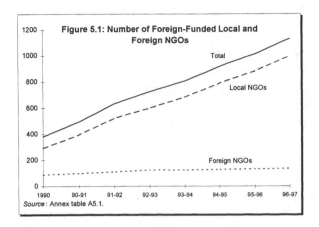

Source: Annex table A5.1.

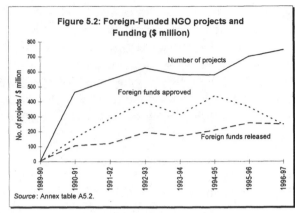

Source: Annex table A5.2.

Microcredit reduces poverty

5.6   The microfinance programs of Grameen Bank and other NGOs lend to groups of poor borrowers in which each group member receives a loan in sequence. No collateral is required and nominal interest rates are around 20 percent. Most borrowers are women. Group-based lending induces self-selection (good credit risks join together) and creates incentives for peer monitoring to reduce the level of group risk. Recent research confirms that microcredit helps to reduce poverty (Khandker and Chowdhury 1996). One recent estimate suggests that the effect of Grameen Bank lending is around 17 cents to the dollar, after controlling for selection bias and nonrandom program placement, meaning that every dollar provided as credit raises annual household expenditures by about 17 cents (Pitt and Khandker 1998). This figure does not include additional earnings that are saved, the value of social education and empowerment, heightened future earnings, and possible spillover effects on non-borrowing households. Microcredit enables borrowers to undertake self-employment in nonfarm activities. The expected gains to poor farm workers joining the nonfarm sector, holding other household characteristics constant, can also be used as a measure (albeit an imperfect one) of the benefits of microcredit programs. Our work suggests that these gains are large, especially for the poorest workers (Background Paper 2).

5.7   *Are microcredit programs sustainable?* This is an area of continuing research but Khandker, Khalily, and Khan (1995) argue that the Grameen Bank's microlending is sustainable because its borrowers are viable: loans have a positive effect on wages, dropout rates are low at about 5 percent, and repayment is above 90 percent. They find that the marginal cost of additional loans is below their marginal revenue, so that Grameen Bank branches acting as semi-independent profit maximizers could improve their financial performance by lending more. However, administrative overheads have been high because of the small average loan size. Grameen Bank has received substantial subsidies from foreign donors and Bangladesh Bank. In 1991-92, these subsidies amounted to about 22 cents for every dollar lent (Ray 1998). Ray suggests that this figure, when compared to the 17 cents of (short-run and partial) benefits created for borrowing households, implies that the cost of targeting the poor by NGOs is about 5 cents, which appears to be quite reasonable. Another way of looking at viability is to consider what interest rates Grameen Bank would have had to charge to cover its administrative expenses and cost of funds. Morduch (1997) has estimated that Grameen Bank would have had to charge interest rates of 32 to 45 percent during 1987-94 (instead of the 12-17 percent that it actually charged) to cover its subsidized borrowing from Bangladesh Bank. Similarly, it would have had to charge interest rates of 18 to 22 percent to cover its grant-subsidized operating costs.

5.8   *Should the government be directly involved in providing microcredit?* The evaluation of the RD-12 program of BRDB by Khandker, Khan, and Khalily (1995) is not as favorable as the evaluation of Grameen Bank, but the authors recommend that the program be continued, in part to foster efficiency through competition between microcredit providers. The government also intervenes through the Palli Karma Sahayak Foundation (PKSF), a quasi-public apex organization channeling funds for microcredit to smaller NGOs that do not have easy access to foreign or local funding. PKSF receives a large part of its funding from abroad, including from a $105 million IDA credit granted in 1996. Rahman (1996) found that loans made by PKSF's partner organizations had a positive impact on standards of living.

Users have the least complaints about NGO-run rural health and education facilities

5.9   How do the users of rural health and education facilities view NGOs, the government, and the private sector as alternative suppliers? The rural community module of the 1995-96 HES offers new insights. The module includes data (obtained from a village head or elected representative) on the top two complaints at the village level about government, NGO, and private health and education facilities.

5.10   *Health facilities.* Poor quality of service and lack of medicines are the top two complaints against government facilities in most villages (table 5.1). A complaint about government facilities being too far is the third most frequent. The primary need in public health from the rural user's point of view appears to be improvement of the quality of public services. Private facilities score better in many complaint areas, but most villages consider them to be too expensive. Also, many people feel that they are too far. NGOs perform better all around with between half and one-third of the villages voicing no complaints. The main complaint against NGO facilities is their distance from villages, suggesting that more and nearer facilities would be welcomed.

Table 5.1: Top Two Complaints about Health Facilities in Rural Villages, 1995-96
(complaints as a percentage of total number of villages responding to the question)

Type of complaint	Government		Private		NGO	
	First	*Second*	*First*	*Second*	*First*	*Second*
Poor quality of service	39.8	12.0	5.2	7.1	3.0	2.6
Lack of courtesy/help	5.0	10.7	1.3	0.9	0.6	0.0
Too expensive	2.5	4.3	77.7	18.8	4.7	3.3
Absence of doctor	2.5	12.0	0.9	5.8	1.8	4.6
Lack of medicines	33.2	39.7	1.8	7.1	5.3	5.2
Long queues/long wait	2.5	6.8	0.9	4.5	8.9	9.1
Too far	11.2	11.5	7.0	34.4	34.9	20.1
Other complaints	0.4	1.3	0.4	8.0	14.2	22.9
No complaints	2.9	1.7	4.8	13.4	26.0	33.1
All Complaints	100.0	100.0	100.0	100.0	100.0	100.0
Number of villages	241	234	229	224	169	154

Note: Percentages are not weighted by village population, and may not add up to 100 percent due to rounding or coding.
Source: World Bank staff estimates using 1995-96 HES.

5.11   *Education facilities.* We can obtain similar, user-oriented insights about the provision of education services. The chief complaint about government education services in most villages is the shortage of primary and secondary government schools, followed by the shortage of teaching staff, and poor teaching quality (table 5.2). There are twice as many villages with the top complaint related to the number of education facilities as to the quality and quantity of teachers, the second biggest complaint. This suggests that both quantity and quality concerns will have to be balanced in the future. Private schools do slightly better on quality, but they are considered too expensive and too far to attend in many villages. NGO schools do better than both government and private schools. One-third villages have no complaints about NGO facilities. For NGOs, the biggest complaints were that NGO schools are too far, followed by the insufficient number of primary and post-primary NGO schools.

5.12   Several conclusions can be drawn from these survey results. First, NGO institutional and incentive structures provide much higher service quality. This calls for scaling up NGO activities and for greater public-NGO partnerships in service delivery. Second, community influence and participation, hallmarks of NGO activities, must be integrated more fully into public service provision to create the conditions under which public services can also become much more responsive to user needs.

Table 5.2: Top Two Complaints about Education Facilities in Rural Villages, 1995-96
(complaints as percentage of total number of villages responding to the question)

Complaint	Government		Private		NGO	
	First	Second	First	Second	First	Second
Not enough institutions (up to primary)	29.5	3.1	12.6	1.3	9.0	3.0
Not enough institutions (post-primary)	15.4	10.1	9.7	4.4	7.1	6.7
Not enough girls-only institutions (up to primary)	6.6	8.4	6.3	7.6	1.9	0.8
Not enough girls-only institutions (post-primary)	8.3	10.6	6.9	5.0	2.6	3.0
Difficulty in admission/enrollment	0.8	1.3	0.6	1.7	1.9	4.5
Poor quality of teaching	10.4	10.6	6.9	8.8	5.8	6.7
Insufficient teaching staff	11.2	18.1	7.4	7.6	5.2	8.2
Too few women teachers	0.8	4.9	1.7	4.4	3.2	1.5
Poor infrastructure in schools	3.7	10.1	4.0	5.0	7.7	9.0
Too expensive	2.1	4.0	17.1	18.9	0.0	6.0
Too far	0.0	4.9	8.0	14.5	18.1	8.2
Very high failure/repetition rates	0.4	1.3	0.6	1.3	0.0	3.0
Schools closed too often	0.4	0.9	2.3	3.8	1.3	1.5
Other complaints	0.4	3.1	1.7	3.8	5.8	6.0
No complaints	10.0	8.8	14.3	12.6	30.3	32.2
All complaints	100.00	100.0	100.0	100.0	100.0	100.0
Number of villages	241	227	175	159	155	134

Note: Percentages are not weighted by village population, and may not add up to 100 percent due to rounding or coding.
Source: World Bank staff estimates using 1995-96 HES.

REACHING THE POOR THROUGH NGO PROGRAMS

5.13   NGOs contribute to development and poverty alleviation in Bangladesh on a scale that is unique in the world. In the face of Bangladesh's poverty and institutional challenges, the success, strengths, and size of NGOs pose the obvious question of whether they can and should be doing more for poverty alleviation. These include questions such as: Does greater competition in microfinance raises any concerns? What should be the role of microfinance in Bangladesh's poverty reduction strategy? Should NGOs reach the rural poorest and those not normally eligible for microcredit? Are there geographic imbalances in the placement of NGO programs? Can land ownership as an indicator be supplemented to improve targeting? We deal with these questions below.

5.14   *Increasing competition in microfinance should increase efficieny, but must not reduce inclusiveness..* The growth of microcredit, including the expansion of PKSF's activities, is likely to increase competition, both among NGOs and with other formal and quasi-formal providers. There are issues of banking regulation and supervision that are being examined in this context, but leaving these aside, there is still a larger issue of the poverty impact of microfinance. It is clear that greater competition will improve efficiency at one level, but it may also pressure NGOs to select less risky clients, meaning that the very poor may be left out. To put it differently, with the high growth in lending it will be important to ensure that quantitative objectives (lending to as many households as possible) are not pursued at the cost of qualitative objectives (lending to households that need credit the most).

Should NGO microfinance reach the poorest and the not-so-poor?

5.15   During the past decade NGOs have grown rapidly to meet the demand for their services from a population with so many deprived members that, in the beginning, it did not matter who among the poor was helped. But given the sophistication and increasing coverage of NGOs, there is now a question of whether NGOs should focus on reaching specific groups among the poor, for example, the poorest. There may also be the need to form partnerships with the government and others to address the credit needs of smaller entrepreneurs, the "missing middle," who do not qualify for microcredit but are yet too small for formal credit. There are opposing views here: one maintains that microcredit should not cater to the poorest because the poorest are not bankable; the other maintains that NGOs have a clear *comparative* advantage in grass-roots and community level activity as compared to public agencies and should therefore try to reach those who are normally excluded by markets or inefficient public systems.

5.16   The strong focus of many NGOs on microcredit may pose special problems related to reaching the poorest. Group lending may exclude the poorest because they represent too big a risk to a group or because they may not have the skills required to participate. At the other end, borrowers in agriculture or nonfarm occupations who are ineligible for microcredit (because they own more than 0.5 acres of land) may still lack access to formal credit markets. Since these entrepreneurs are likely to be more interested in generating wage employment rather than self-employment, they represent different types of risk. Group-based microcredit lending may not be the strategy and right financial intermediation for this group, which in many countries has formed the basis for dynamic growth.

5.17   Land-based targeting (discussed below) does not ensure that NGOs reach the poorest. For example, the Association for Social Advancement (ASA 1997) identified a number of factors preventing the chronic poor from joining its programs. These include inappropriate guidelines issued by the central office for selecting program participants and constraints faced by the poorest themselves, such as lack of clothing or initial savings, to participate in group meetings. Pooling of group risks also creates incentives for groups to exclude the most risky participants.

5.18   The above considerations suggest a market segmentation of the rural borrowers and the type of NGO partnerships that could cater to different segments of the market (Figure 5.3). Mainstream NGOs would provide microfinance to their usual borrowers—those marginal landowners and the landless who possess entrepreneurial and other self-employment skills to self-select themselves into microcredit groups. Below these borrowers are two large segments consisting of poorer potential borrowers and the indigent. The potentially very large pool of poorer borrowers are those who do not as yet have the immediate abilities or the motivation to be able to join a credit group and benefit from microcredit. Some form of venture or risk capital is likely to be needed to finance programs to assist these borrowers, possibly also run by NGOs in partnerships with the government and donors. These programs could be designed to specifically cater to the skill-building needs of the marginal borrowers as well as to accommodate the higher risks these borrowers are likely to represent. The long-term indigent are unlikely to be able to benefit from credit, but need support from safety nets. In practice, these market segments are of course a continuum of clients and credit providers with overlapping coverage (figure 5.3).

Figure 5.3: Reaching the Rural Poor

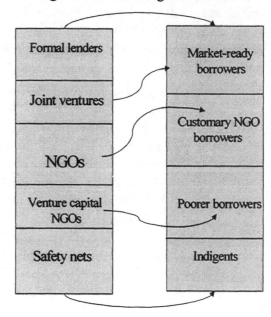

5.19   Few would disagree that microcredit is helping to reduce poverty in Bangladesh. But few would argue that it can be relied on as the only or principal means of poverty reduction. These considerations suggest that microcredit can and should be a vital element of a poverty reduction strategy of inclusive, rapid growth, even though it is unlikely to be the panacea for poverty reduction.

Land ownership targets the poor, but could be supplemented by village-level targeting

5.20   Targeting enables policymakers to maximize the effectiveness of their limited resources by focusing programs on the poor. Several household characteristics can be used as targeting indicators. In Bangladesh, NGOs and the government have predominantly used land ownership (with a typical threshold of 0.5 acres) to screen participants. This has a number of attractive properties. *First*, rising land ownership is strongly correlated with lowering poverty, which makes it less likely to select a nonpoor household or to reject a poor household on the basis of the land it owns (Background Paper 6). *Second*, the administrative costs of selecting households tend to be low because it is relatively easy to identify the landless and marginal land owners. *Third*, targeting through land ownershop is unlikely to distort the decision to own land because being a rural landowner in Bangladesh is usually not a matter of choice but more the result of inheritance. Nonetheless, some research does suggests that targeting could be improved by supplementing landownership with other indicators (Ravallion and Sen 1994). In fact, some NGOs use a combination of landownership, number of days employed, and (for women) desertion and widow as targeting indicators.

5.21   *Village-level targeting may offer other means to reach the poorest.* Village and area effects on living standards are large in Bangladesh. It may therefore be possible to reach the poorest by targeting poorer villages, as opposed to targeting the poor in all villages. Since many villages (poor or rich) now have NGO and/or government offices, as a practical matter, there may already be limits to village-level targeting, though this could be compensated to some degree by the relative allocation of NGO resources and the size of operations in poorer villages.

5.22   According to data from the 1995-96 HES, neither government nor NGO programs appear to be well targeted at the village level in rural areas. Table 5.3 shows that nonpoor villages are as likely as poor villages to benefit from government and NGO programs with the possible exception of Vulnerable Group Development. For example, of all villages benefiting from Food For Work, 53 percent are poor, while 47 percent are nonpoor.

Table 5.3: Village Targeting of Government and NGO Programs in Rural Areas, 1995-96

(percent)

Village type	Share of government programs by village type			Share of NGO programs by village type		
	FFW	VGD	FFE	Grameen	BRAC	Others
Poor (50)	53	64	50	49	52	57
Nonpoor (50)	47	36	50	51	48	43

Note: Villages with mean per capita consumption below the median for all villages are considered poor, while villages with mean per capita consumption above the median are considered nonpoor. Hence there are as many poor as nonpoor villages. This definition is a matter of convenience; another definition would not affect the results in terms of targeting.

Source: World Bank staff estimates using 1995-96 HES.

5.23   What would be the potential benefit of focusing programs on poor villages? Simulations based on Food for Education (which is not an NGO program) indicate that the share of nonpoor households (identified by the upper poverty lines) benefiting from the program could be cut in half—from one-third to one-sixth of beneficiary households—if only poor villages were offered the program (poor villages have a higher proportion of poor households). The gains are similar using the lower poverty lines. Reaping these gains would require finding ways to identify poor villages. This may not be easy, and further research is warranted to better understand the dynamics of NGO and government program placement at the village level.

SUMMARY

5.24   Bangladesh is known internationally for its innovative NGOs, which have grown rapidly. The number of NGOs registered with the NGO Affairs Bureau has tripled since 1990. In some areas the size of NGO programs is now on a par with the size of government programs. While the influence of NGOs and their reliance on foreign funding has been a source of tension with the government in the past, the situation has improved and partnerships with NGOs are now very common. This collaboration should be encouraged further since it benefits the poor.

5.25   Microcredit programs such as those provided by BRAC, ASA, Proshika, and the Grameen Bank are among the best known, but NGOs are active in many other areas, including education and health care. NGO activities reduce poverty. While standards of living are best measured by comparing consumption to a poverty line, poverty is inherently multidimensional. Other important dimensions of well-being besides consumption include those related to employment opportunities, gender issues, and access to basic social services. The impact of NGOs in these areas is positive as well. For example, NGOs facilities receive less complaints than government and private facilities.

5.26   The focus of many NGOs on microcredit may pose special problems related to reaching the poorest. There may also be the need to form partnerships with the government and others to address the credit needs of the small entrepreneurs who do not qualify for microcredit but are yet too small for formal credit.

Estimating the cost of basic needs poverty lines in Bangladesh

1.   This note describes the cost of basic needs method used to estimate poverty lines for the 1995-96 HES (BBS 1997e and Background Papers 4 and 5). Acknowledging the fact that prices may differ by geographical area, poverty lines were computed at a more disaggregated level than the urban-rural split, specifically for 14 geographical areas (6 urban and 8 rural: table A1.0). Three steps were followed.

2.   First, a food bundle $(F_1, ... F_N)$ providing 2,122 kcal per day per person was chosen. The food bundle corresponds to actual consumption patterns in the country. It comprises rice, wheat, pulses, milk, mustard oil, beef, fresh water fish, potato, other vegetables, sugar and bananas (table A1.1). In each of the 14 geographical areas, the price of each item in the bundle was estimated. It is known that richer households buy better and more expensive food than poor households. Hence, not controlling for household characteristics may yield upward biases in the estimated food prices. Therefore, regressions were used to find the prices paid by the poor, controlling for total consumption, education, and occupation. Given the estimates of the food prices by area, food poverty lines were computed as $Z_{fk} = \Sigma_j P_{jk} F_j$, where F_j is the per capita quantity of food item j in the bundle (common for all areas) and P_{jk} is the price of j in area k. The prices are given in table A1.1 by area for 1995-96.

3.   The second step is to compute the cost of basic nonfood needs. The approach used for basic food needs cannot be followed here because there is no widely agreed on basket of nonfood goods that can be deemed as essential. And even if there were such a basket of nonfood goods, their prices would be hard to estimate. An alternative approach was proposed by Ravallion (1994). We denote household per capita consumption for household i by y_i and food per capita consumption by x_i. First, in each area k the nonfood expenditures $z^L_{nk} = E[y_i - x_i \mid y_i = z_{fk}]$ among households whose *total* consumption expenditures are equal to their regional food poverty line z_{fk} ($y_i = z_{fk}$) were estimated. Since these households spend less on food than the food poverty line, what they spend on nonfood items must be devoted to bare essentials. The nonfood allowance z^L_{nk} can be considered as a lower bound for the cost of nonfood basic needs. Next, upper bounds for the cost of nonfood basic needs $z^U_{nk} = E[y_i - x_i \mid x_i = z_{fk}]$ were estimated as the nonfood expenditures (in each area) among households whose *food* expenditures are equal to the food poverty line ($x_i = z_{fk}$). In practice, both z^L_{kn} and z^U_{kn} were estimated using a nonparametric technique (Background Paper 4). As the share of consumption expenditures devoted to food typically decreases when consumption increases, z^U_{kn} tends to be larger than z^L_{kn}, which was indeed observed.

4.   The third step consists of summing up the food and lower and upper nonfood allowances to obtain the lower and upper poverty lines by area. In area k, the lower poverty line is defined as $z^L_k = z_{fk} + z^L_{nk}$ and the upper line is $z^U_k = z_{fk} + z^U_{nk}$. The resulting lower and upper poverty lines by geographic area for various years are given in Table A1.2. The food, lower, and upper poverty lines by area are shown for 1995-96 in Figure A1.1. For example, the four highest levels of the upper poverty line are for the Dhaka SMA (Area 1), Other Urban Areas of the Dhaka Division (Area 2), Urban Areas of the Khulna Division (Area 9), and the Chittagong SMA (Area 5).

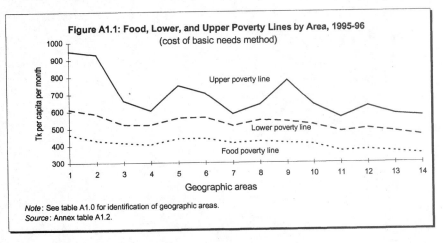

Figure A1.1: Food, Lower, and Upper Poverty Lines by Area, 1995-96
(cost of basic needs method)

Note: See table A1.0 for identification of geographic areas.
Source: Annex table A1.2.

Weaknesses of the Direct Calorie Intake and Food Energy Intake methods for measuring poverty

5.   The direct calorie intake method, as used by the BBS, considers any household with a caloric intake per capita less than 2,122 kcal per day as poor (1,805 kcal for the "hard core" poor). But caloric intake is too narrow an indicator of well-being; it covers only one aspect of welfare (albeit an important one). Households must spend money on other items, such as clothing, shelter, education, and social events. Moreover, caloric intake can be a misleading indicator of nutrition. For example, the share of the population with a caloric intake below 2,122 kcal is similar in urban and rural areas, which might suggest that the prevalence of malnutrition is similar in both areas. However, the Child Nutrition Surveys of the BBS indicate that malnutrition (as measured by wasting and stunting) is much higher in rural areas.

6.   The food energy intake method determines the per capita consumption expenditures in taka at which a household can be expected to fulfill its caloric threshold requirement. This level of expenditure is then the poverty line. Since this welfare indicator (expenditure) is more comprehensive, embracing other goods and services, the food energy intake method is superior to the direct calorie intake method in terms of better representing what people actually consume. But the food energy intake method suffers from major deficiencies when used for poverty comparisons, because the poverty lines it generates do not represent identical purchasing power in real terms over time or across sectors or groups. For example, if tastes differ between rural and urban sectors, with urban consumers preferring to buy more expensive foods to meet the same caloric standard, then the urban poverty line will be higher than the rural poverty line. The same per capita expenditures that put a rural household above the rural poverty line may not place an urban household above the urban poverty line. Thus we would see a higher incidence of urban poverty. In fact, the BBS's food energy intake poverty estimates show a similar incidence of poverty in rural and urban areas, contradicting other evidence that suggests that rural poverty is far more prevalent.

7.   To determine whether poverty has risen or fallen over time, it is important to account for increases or decreases in households' command over commodities. Food energy intake poverty lines may not reflect this well. For example, using this method the 1988-89 urban poverty line (Tk 500 a month per person) computed by the BBS is *lower* than the 1985-86 urban poverty line (Tk 519 a month per person), although prices of most consumption commodities increased between the two years. The 1988-89 urban poverty line was lower because it did not represent the same standard of living as the 1985-86 urban poverty line. Basing poverty comparisons on poverty lines that do not represent similar levels of well being over time and space can be seriously misleading. Such poverty lines may indicate that the incidence of poverty has decreased while it has actually increased, or the other way around (see Background Papers 4 and 6 and Ravallion 1994).

ANNEX TABLES

Table A1.0: Area Definitions for Estimating Poverty Incidence

Areas	Definition
1	Dhaka SMA
2	Other urban areas of the Dhaka division
3	Rural areas of the Dhaka and Mymensingh districts
4	Rural areas of the Faridpur, Tangail, and Jamalpur districts
5	Chittagong SMA
6	Other urban areas of the Chittagong division
7	Rural areas of the Sylhet and Comilla districts
8	Rural areas of the Noakhali and Chittagong districts
9	Urban areas of the Khulna division
10	Rural areas of the Barisal and Pathuakali districts
11	Rural areas of the Khulna, Jessore, and Kushtia districts
12	Urban areas of the Rajshahi division
13	Rural areas of the Rajshahi and Pabna districts
14	Rural areas of the Bogra, Rangpur, and Dinajpur districts

Table A1.1: Food Prices per Kilogram and Food Poverty Lines in Taka per Person per Month by Geographical Area, 1995-96

	Rice	Wheat	Pulses	Meat	Potatoes	Milk	Oil	Bananas	Sugar	Fish	Vegetables	ZF [a]
Grams/day	391.06	39.40	39.40	11.82	26.60	57.13	19.70	19.70	19.70	47.28	147.76	
Areas[b]												
1	14.25	12.59	39.80	60.60	7.92	19.61	55.33	19.70	35.32	50.06	7.37	465.86
2	12.75	10.92	39.03	61.79	8.55	15.16	55.80	20.61	37.15	46.39	6.15	429.51
3	12.91	10.92	40.00	60.00	8.00	14.67	60.00	13.33	31.82	40.00	6.00	415.68
4	12.44	10.11	39.41	54.84	7.84	13.31	63.54	19.30	31.80	37.57	6.02	406.32
5	13.52	12.00	39.38	72.89	8.74	16.48	65.79	19.49	35.65	38.24	6.53	441.20
6	13.04	11.27	39.74	66.60	8.98	16.06	67.44	26.32	33.86	38.81	7.58	441.83
7	12.73	11.30	38.53	66.66	8.18	15.01	57.92	22.08	34.27	31.93	7.30	415.06
8	12.82	11.60	39.80	68.73	8.59	14.65	60.35	20.06	35.21	40.41	5.94	425.32
9	13.11	10.96	38.98	58.42	8.68	14.07	56.15	18.88	32.74	40.04	5.69	416.08
10	12.90	11.18	37.33	62.87	8.78	13.15	64.05	17.46	34.75	33.17	6.16	409.18
11	12.05	10.30	32.30	52.69	7.96	11.54	56.70	16.39	29.74	33.13	4.04	367.35
12	12.26	10.32	35.51	47.71	6.97	12.98	57.11	16.87	31.24	32.25	4.54	375.98
13	11.18	9.52	36.68	40.45	7.98	12.45	57.35	21.02	30.43	32.75	4.44	363.29
14	11.15	9.74	32.47	47.58	7.42	10.51	55.59	12.38	29.82	32.62	4.32	349.57

[a] ZF is the food poverty line representing the food bundle shown in this table and corresponding to 2,122 kcalories per person per day.
[b] For a definition of the areas see table A1.0

Table A1.2: Food, Lower, and Upper Poverty Lines by Area in Taka per Person per Month, 1983-84 to 1995-96

	1983-84			1985-86			1988-89			1991-92			1995-96		
	ZF	ZL	ZU	ZF	ZL	ZU	ZF	ZL	ZU	ZF	ZL	ZU	ZF	ZL	ZU
Areas[a]															
1	198	254	342	248	331	478	305	401	565	365	480	660	466	613	950
2	192	258	314	234	308	381	293	389	437	317	399	482	430	584	931
3	191	241	279	223	291	336	285	358	405	336	425	512	416	523	661
4	180	231	271	218	282	325	281	344	355	350	432	472	406	521	604
5	197	258	375	238	321	404	305	399	507	384	523	722	441	561	749
6	193	238	291	236	317	400	301	384	475	391	517	609	442	564	704
7	188	241	281	223	291	345	285	368	513	352	432	558	415	515	584
8	195	259	297	231	301	366	287	394	436	341	438	541	425	548	638
9	186	245	302	220	286	401	283	364	473	381	482	635	416	541	779
10	183	234	253	220	280	316	281	355	397	322	413	467	409	522	639
11	183	229	270	210	286	339	266	353	405	328	420	497	367	481	563
12	188	248	351	223	296	384	280	357	462	342	446	582	376	499	628
13	184	238	292	208	282	330	261	333	371	353	459	540	363	480	582
14	181	238	302	204	272	303	270	347	386	336	426	487	350	457	570

[a] For a definition of the areas see table A1.0

Note: ZF is the food poverty line; ZL is the lower poverty line; ZU is the upper poverty line.

Table A1.3: Gini Indices of Inequality, 1983-84 to 1995-96

	Normalization by lower poverty lines					Normalization by upper poverty lines				
	1983-84	1985-86	1988-89	1991-92	1995-96	1983-84	1985-86	1988-89	1991-92	1995-96
Gini index										
National	25.53	25.66	27.94	27.15	31.01	25.38	24.73	27.02	25.92	29.34
Rural	24.33	23.80	25.96	25.06	26.43	24.62	23.58	25.71	24.34	26.47
Urban	29.46	29.87	31.78	31.09	36.03	29.31	29.34	31.35	30.68	35.28
Decomposition										
Within group	24.93	24.64	26.74	25.93	28.02	25.17	24.38	26.46	25.25	27.93
Stratification	-0.29	-0.54	-0.79	-0.84	-1.80	-0.02	-0.01	-0.19	-0.27	-0.52
Between group	0.89	1.56	1.99	2.06	4.79	0.23	0.36	0.75	0.94	1.93

Note: The between group component measures the inequality between urban and rural areas, while the within group component measures the inequality within urban and rural areas. Stratification is a measure of overlap between urban and rural areas in the distribution of consumption. The measures of per capita consumption used to compute the Gini index are normalized by the cost of basic needs poverty lines (lower and upper) in order to account for differences in costs of living between geographical areas.
Source: World Bank staff estimates.

Table A1.4: Regional Poverty Profile by Administrative Division, 1995-96
(percentage of the population below the poverty line)

	Very poor (lower poverty lines)					Poor (upper poverty lines)				
	Barisal	Chittagong	Dhaka	Khulna	Rajshahi	Barisal	Chittagong	Dhaka	Khulna	Rajshahi
Headcount										
Division	43.9	32.4	33.0	32.2	41.6	59.9	44.9	52.0	51.7	62.2
Rural	44.8	35.3	41.5	33.2	44.4	60.6	47.2	58.9	51.5	65.7
Urban	28.9	12.1	10.8	25.8	19.2	47.7	29.2	33.6	53.3	33.9
Share of the poor										
Division	8.6	23.8	28.8	10.9	27.9	7.9	22.2	30.3	11.7	27.9
Rural	8.3	22.7	26.2	9.7	26.4	7.5	20.3	24.9	10.1	26.2
Urban	0.3	1.1	2.6	1.2	1.4	0.4	1.8	5.4	1.6	1.7

Source: BBS (1997e).

Table A1.5: Headcount Index by Education of Household Head, 1995-96
(percentage of the population below the poverty line)

	Very poor (lower poverty lines)				Poor (upper poverty lines)			
	No School	Class 1-4	Class 5-9	SSC & above	No school	Class 1-4	Class 5-9	SSC & above
National	48.0	30.6	22.7	6.9	67.0	49.9	40.5	15.5
Rural	50.1	33.0	25.8	11.0	67.5	50.7	42.7	22.8
Urban	29.0	16.2	10.7	1.7	62.3	44.8	31.7	6.3

Source: BBS (1997e). SSC= secondary school certificate.

Table A1.6: Headcount Index by Land Ownership in Acres, 1995-96
(percentage of the population below the poverty line)

	All sizes	Landless	Below 0.05	0.05 to 0.49	0.50 to 1.49	1.50 to 2.49	2.50 to 7.49	7.50 or more
	Very poor (lower poverty lines)							
National	35.6	39.9	50.5	47.0	30.9	21.4	16.0	2.4
Rural	39.8	57.9	63.1	53.1	33.5	22.9	17.4	2.6
Urban	14.3	19.4	22.1	13.2	4.5	3.6	0.6	0.0
	Poor (upper poverty lines)							
National	53.1	58.2	68.9	64.2	51.0	40.6	30.9	9.3
Rural	56.7	69.0	80.0	69.8	53.6	42.8	32.4	9.1
Urban	35.0	45.8	43.6	32.9	24.2	13.8	13.1	11.0

Source: BBS (1997e).

Table A2.1: Simulated Headcount Index with Changes in Growth and Inequality, 1983-84 to 1995-96

	Very poor (lower poverty lines)					Poor (upper poverty lines)				
	1983-84	1985-86	1988-89	1991-92	1995-96	1983-84	1985-86	1988-89	1991-92	1995-96
National										
Actual headcount	40.91	33.77	41.32	42.69	35.55	58.50	51.73	57.13	58.84	53.08
"Growth" headcount	-	32.01	36.65	39.79	25.90	-	49.03	52.62	59.24	46.34
"Inequality" headcount	-	43.99	45.18	43.70	50.51	-	60.32	62.32	58.14	64.00
Rural										
Actual headcount	42.62	36.01	44.30	45.95	39.76	59.61	53.14	59.18	61.19	56.65
"Growth" headcount	-	29.37	41.18	44.44	35.05	-	48.51	56.03	62.94	53.06
"Inequality" headcount	-	44.36	45.88	44.30	47.53	-	60.91	62.78	58.41	62.79
Urban										
Actual headcount	28.03	19.90	21.99	23.29	14.32	50.15	42.92	43.88	44.87	35.04
"Growth" headcount	-	22.32	18.97	21.44	7.96	-	41.35	37.46	41.25	26.42
"Inequality" headcount	-	29.07	32.30	29.70	37.84	-	50.94	53.65	51.50	55.90

Note: The "growth only" scenario is based on actual growth with no change in inequality. The "inequality only" scenario is based on actual changes in inequality with zero growth.
Source: World Bank staff estimates.

Table A2.2: Elasticity of Poverty Measures with Respect to Growth and Inequality, 1983-84 to 1995-96

	Lower poverty line			Upper poverty line		
	Net impact of growth	Impact of growth controlling for inequality	Impact of inequality controlling for growth	Net impact of growth	Impact of growth controlling for inequality	Impact of inequality controlling for growth
Headcount	-1.98	-2.42	1.28	-1.29	-1.43	0.52
Poverty gap	-2.67	-3.47	2.30	-2.17	-2.57	1.49
Squared poverty gap	-3.30	-4.39	3.12	-2.85	-3.44	2.18

Note: These estimates use a panel of poverty measures at the regional level. The net impact of growth on poverty is the impact after netting out the impact of the increase in inequality on poverty.
Source: World Bank staff estimates.

Table A2.3: Poverty Simulations under Alternative Growth Scenarios, 1996 to 2008

	Poverty incidence in 1996	Poverty incidence in 2008		
		Base case growth	Higher growth via services	Higher growth via agriculture
National				
Headcount	35.56	22.85	22.30	20.28
Squared poverty gap	2.59	1.04	1.00	0.76
Agriculture				
Headcount	41.26	31.46	31.46	26.20
Squared poverty gap	3.12	1.55	1.55	0.95
Industry				
Headcount	36.49	18.74	17.94	16.72
Squared poverty gap	1.97	0.44	0.39	0.32
Services				
Headcount	28.72	15.01	13.97	15.34
Squared poverty gap	2.59	0.64	0.56	0.66

Source: World Bank staff estimates.

Table A3.1: Percentage Gains in Per Capita Consumption from Education, 1983-84 to 1995-96
(gains are measured relative to consumption of households in which household head and spouse have no schooling)

	Urban areas					Rural areas				
	1983-84	1985-86	1988-89	1991-92	1995-96	1983-84	1985-86	1988-89	1991-92	1995-96
Household head										
Some primary	2.51	9.40	-	14.96	13.46	11.79	10.91	-	6.23	6.19
Primary completed	20.03	17.78	9.00	13.93	18.84	15.22	12.91	9.01	8.00	7.27
Some secondary	18.75	25.79	15.71	24.65	23.68	17.05	16.12	18.65	10.39	12.65
Secondary completed	25.90	38.00	34.82	37.15	47.87	32.65	30.16	21.01	16.01	17.35
Spouse										
Some primary	8.10	11.17	-	4.20	3.13	4.93	0.06	-	5.04	4.32
Primary completed	13.07	12.87	2.09	8.38	8.11	-0.78	7.21	3.54	11.92	9.21
Some secondary	20.35	23.34	15.14	15.01	16.39	11.44	15.17	9.41	16.94	22.16
Secondary completed	43.32	43.43	39.84	38.13	41.82	28.98	40.66	19.45	25.11	39.41

Note: The definition of the education levels is slightly different for the 1988-89 HES. The gains for 1983-84 and 1985-86 may be overestimated due to omitted variable bias because land information is not available for these years. The gains are slightly higher when taking into account occupational choice.
Source: World Bank staff estimates.

Table A3.2: Percentage Gains in Per Capita Consumption by Occupation of the Household Head, 1988-89 to 1995-96
(gains are measured relative to consumption of households with household heads working as landless agricultural workers)

	Urban areas			Rural areas		
	1988-89	1991-92	1995-96	1988-89	1991-92	1995-96
Agriculture						
Agricultural worker with land	16.49	12.32	2.40	9.38	9.51	10.76
Worker in fisheries, livestock, forestry	10.75	30.42	16.18	16.02	16.68	15.70
Tenant farmer	15.42	26.69	20.49	17.75	18.96	18.23
Owner farmer	21.89	34.42	32.69	14.07	17.55	23.46
Nonagriculture						
Servant, day-laborer	15.88	16.46	10.57	8.74	8.71	11.24
Transport, communication worker	7.98	25.43	17.20	21.59	19.13	19.06
Salesman, services, broker	13.85	19.25	22.07	21.91	19.14	22.15
Factory worker, artisan	24.40	29.73	22.15	20.86	14.88	20.28
Petty trader, small businessman	34.68	36.59	34.06	24.21	25.46	28.70
Executive, official, teacher	20.02	29.98	27.44	23.84	26.46	23.79
Retired, student, not working	17.10	35.48	25.49	12.43	10.17	21.99

Note: The gains are not shown for 1983-84 and 1985-86 because of differences in the definition of occupations for these years.
Source: World Bank staff estimates.

Table A3.3: Percentage Gains in Consumption from Land Ownership, 1988-89 to 1995-96
(gain is measured relative to the per capita consumption of a landless household)

	Urban areas			Rural areas		
	1988-89	*1991-92*	*1995-96*	*1988-89*	*1991-92*	*1995-96*
Acres of land						
0.05 to 0.49	9.76	8.60	10.39	8.66	7.91	7.04
0.50 to 1.49	7.84	8.20	9.56	13.23	17.11	15.83
1.50 to 2.49	15.29	10.14	19.05	21.90	28.18	22.99
2.50 or more	21.69	26.82	24.24	39.86	41.99	42.81

Source: World Bank staff estimates. Land ownership data are not available in the 1983-84 and 1985-86 HES.

Table A3.4: Trends in Real Wages by Sector, 1983-1996
(1970 = 100)

Fiscal year	General	Agriculture	Manufacturing	Construction
1983	88	82	82	99
1984	90	70	95	99
1985	86	70	91	91
1986	95	80	102	100
1987	102	86	109	106
1988	106	89	108	117
1989	107	89	110	120
1990	110	94	115	113
1991	107	91	114	107
1992	107	93	113	104
1993	113	99	119	109
1994	114	101	121	106
1995	111	98	121	100
1996	114	97	123	105
Ratio 1996/1983	1.30	1.18	1.50	1.06

Source: CIRDAP (1997c).

Table A3.5: Unemployment and Underemployment, 1995-96

	Bangladesh			Urban			Rural		
	All	*Men*	*Women*	*All*	*Men*	*Women*	*All*	*Men*	*Women*
Population (million)									
1. Labor force	56.0	34.7	21.3	10.2	7.4	2.8	45.8	27.3	18.5
2. Unemployed	1.4	0.9	0.5	0.5	0.3	0.1	1.0	0.6	0.4
3. Work ≤15 hours	7.8	1.5	6.3	0.7	0.1	0.6	7.1	1.4	5.7
4. Employed =(1)-(2)	54.6	33.8	20.8	9.7	7.0	2.7	44.8	26.7	18.1
5. Work ≤35 hours	18.9	4.2	14.7	1.9	0.7	1.2	17.0	3.5	13.5
Rates (%)									
Unemployment (2)/(1)	2.5	2.6	2.3	4.9	4.1	3.6	2.2	2.2	2.2
[(2)+(3)]/(1)	16.5	7.1	31.7	11.3	6.2	24.5	17.6	7.4	32.8
Underemployment (5)/(4)	34.6	12.4	70.7	19.6	10.0	44.4	37.9	13.1	74.6

Note: Numbers may not add up due to rounding.
Source: 1995-96 Labor Force Survey (BBS 1996b).

Table A3.6: Unemployment by Education Level for Population 15 Years and Older, 1995-96

	Bangladesh			Urban			Rural		
	All	*Men*	*Women*	*All*	*Men*	*Women*	*All*	*Man*	*Women*
Unemployed (thousands)									
Total	1,266	848	418	401	299	102	865	549	316
No education	180	84	96	45	27	18	136	58	78
Class I-X	600	390	210	186	141	45	416	250	166
SSC, HSC, and equivalent	360	273	87	107	87	20	253	186	67
Degree and above	125	100	25	64	45	19	61	56	6
Unemployment rate (%)									
Total	2.5	2.7	2.2	4.4	4.4	4.3	2.1	2.2	1.9
No education	0.7	0.6	0.8	1.5	1.5	1.6	0.6	0.5	0.7
Class I-X	3.0	2.9	3.3	4.6	4.5	5.0	2.6	2.4	3.0
SSC, HSC, and equivalent	10.3	9.7	12.9	7.9	7.8	8.8	11.8	10.9	15.0
Degree and above	9.2	8.4	15.2	7.3	6.0	15.3	12.7	12.7	15.4

Note: Numbers may not add up due to rounding.
Source: 1995-96 Labor Force Survey (BBS 1996b).

Table A3.7: Impact of Area Characteristics on Differences in Poverty between Greater Districts, 1991-92
(lower poverty line)

	Urban areas			Rural areas		
	Observed headcount	*Geographic profile*	*Concentration profile*	*Observed headcount*	*Geographic profile*	*Concentration profile*
Dhaka	13.47	12.50	34.73	39.48	24.23	48.44
Mymensingh	32.89	27.13	40.26	52.19	48.58	48.66
Faridpur	51.56	43.60	48.56	64.25	61.03	49.88
Tangail/Jam.	50.00	65.11	37.35	58.58	60.41	49.75
Chittagong	16.97	16.16	38.03	20.00	13.61	55.02
Comilla	37.50	36.77	40.56	34.80	28.31	48.04
Sylhet	12.50	10.46	57.09	10.78	8.85	49.57
Noakhali	37.50	59.39	27.78	37.36	28.70	47.80
Khulna	27.08	2 7.09	30.41	48.57	43.41	43.87
Jessore	21.88	30.10	33.91	35.79	26.37	48.71
Barisal/Pat.	40.63	47.29	28.68	52.49	49.23	45.73
Kushtia	34.38	40.27	36.06	38.54	35.62	45.63
Rajshahi	18.75	35.59	29.30	55.35	53.53	49.25
Rangpur	28.13	34.83	38.52	65.30	62.00	54.63
Pabna	27.91	34.18	36.77	62.50	48.22	58.19
Dinajpur	37.10	40.84	41.40	55.11	41.97	54.02
Bogra	37.50	25.99	58.14	51.75	48.42	48.21

Note: Differences between districts in the poverty in the geographic profile are due to area characteristics. Differences in the concentration profile are due to differences in household characteristics.
Source: World Bank staff estimates using the 1991-92 HES.

Table A3.8: Contribution of Area and Household Characteristics to Inequality, 1983-84 to 1995-96
(the contribution of each set of variables is obtained holding other variables constant)

	Urban areas					Rural areas				
	1983-84	*1985-86*	*1988-89*	*1991-92*	*1995-96*	*1983-84*	*1985-86*	*1988-89*	*1991-92*	*1995-96*
Overall Gini	29.46	29.87	31.78	31.09	36.03	24.33	23.80	25.96	25.06	26.43
Location	8.38	7.60	7.28	8.74	9.24	5.85	7.49	5.55	10.77	6.48
Educ. Head	6.09	8.54	7.78	8.11	10.86	5.16	4.91	3.96	2.66	2.90
Educ. Spouse	7.18	7.49	6.37	6.57	6.78	1.24	1.61	1.09	2.19	2.66
Occup. Head	5.76	3.67	5.03	4.34	4.52	7.29	6.84	4.55	4.37	4.62
Land	-	-	3.95	3.71	3.90	-	-	7.51	7.98	7.33

Note: The contributions of groups of variables need not add up to the overall Gini. The conditional between group inequality for land cannot be estimated with the 1983-84 and 1985-86 HES data sets.
Source: World Bank staff estimates.

Table A4.1. Annual Development Program: Social Sector Expenditures in Constant Prices
(billion taka in 1995-96 prices)

Spending category	Fiscal year 1990	Percentage of ADP	Fiscal year 1996	Percentage of ADP	Fiscal year 2001 (planned)	Percentage of ADP
Total social expenditures	7.93	9.95	28.54	24.39	45.45	29.43
Education	3.15	3.96	15.88	13.57	23.88	15.45
Health	1.37	1.71	5.85	5.00	13.80	8.93
Family Planning	3.07	3.85	4.94	4.22	4.83	3.12
Social Welfare	0.36	0.45	1.87	1.60	2.98	1.93
Total ADP	71.75	100.00	117.00	100.00	154.52	100.00

Note: Education includes spending for religion in 1996 and 2001. Sports and culture not included.
Source: World Bank (1996) for 1990, and BBS (1997: III-12) for other years.

Table A4.2. Rural Income Distribution and Benefits from Public Spending on Health, 1994

Per capita income decile	Share of rural income	Share of benefits from public spending on health
1	1.94	12.88
2	3.25	8.86
3	4.11	12.22
4	5.64	3.67
5	6.05	17.84
6	6.91	8.13
7	9.50	8.62
8	12.63	6.87
9	17.38	7.27
10	32.59	13.64
Total	100.00	100.00

Note: Numbers may not add up due to rounding.
Source: CIRDAP (1997a).

Table A4.3. Rural Income Distribution and Benefits from Public Spending on Education, 1994

Per capita income decile	Share of rural income	Share of benefits from public spending on education			
		Primary	Secondary	Higher	Total
1	1.94	9.53	3.04	0.76	6.87
2	3.25	9.89	3.04	0.76	7.00
3	4.11	9.35	5.12	3.03	7.34
4	5.64	9.89	7.02	3.03	8.71
5	6.05	9.53	7.97	6.81	8.49
6	6.91	10.06	10.06	4.54	8.18
7	9.50	10.43	13.09	13.64	11.31
8	12.63	10.43	15.75	18.94	13.27
9	17.38	10.62	17.08	19.70	13.41
10	32.59	10.27	17.83	28.79	15.42
Total	100.00	100.00	100.00	100.00	100.00

Note: Numbers may not add up due to rounding.
Source: CIRDAP (1997b).

Table A4.4: Food Grain Distribution under Government Programs
(thousand tons)

Program	1990-91	1991-92	1992-93	1993-94	1994-95	1995-96
Wheat total	604	834	253	774	999	1078
FFW	420	512	164	424	493	468
FFE	-	-	-	79	168	237
VGD	139	204	76	167	182	172
Test relief	32	94	3	71	92	88
Others	13	24	10	32	64	112
Rice total	194	91	365	71	66	70
Grain total	798	925	618	845	1065	1148

Note: FFE is Food for Education and was started in 1993; FFW is Food for Work; VGD is Vulnerable Group Development
Source: World Food Programme, Dhaka.

Table A4.5: Targeting Performance of Selected Food Safety Nets, 1991

Household	Rural population	Population share in 1991 surveys on food safety nets		
Income group (Tk)	Share in 1991-92 HES	FFW	VGD	Test Relief
<750	3.18	31.85	54.42	27.63
750-999	4.06	22.11	22.87	20.15
1000-1249	7.24	19.40	10.75	17.03
1250-1499	7.60	10.74	5.29	10.51
1500-1999	16.38	9.38	3.68	13.52
2000-2499	12.99	3.81	2.13	6.65
2500-2999	10.26	1.66	0.63	3.09
3000+	38.29	1.09	0.23	1.42
Total	100.00	100.00	100.00	100.00

Note: Income groups defined in taka per household per month. Population shares based on number of households by category without weighting by household size. Numbers may not add up due to rounding. Methodologies differ among cited surveys.
Source: BBS reports on Food For Work, Vulnerable Good Development, Test Relief Surveys for 1991, and HES for 1991-92.

Table A5.1. Number of Foreign-funded NGOs Registered with NGO Affairs Bureau, 1990-98

Period	Local NGOs		Foreign NGOs		Total NGOs	
	New	Cumulative	New	Cumulative	New	Cumulative
1990	293	293	89	89	382	382
1990-91	102	395	10	99	112	494
1991-92	129	523	12	111	141	634
1992-93	77	600	14	125	91	725
1993-94	106	683	9	124	115	807
1994-95	108	790	5	129	113	919
1995-96	92	882	3	132	95	1014
1996-97	115	997	3	135	118	1132
1997-98 (through Nov. 97)	48	1045	5	140	53	1185

Note: Bureau was set up in 1990, so earlier data not available. Cumulative figures show data for existing projects, plus new projects, and less completed projects.
Source: NGO Affairs Bureau.

Table A5.2. Foreign-funded NGO Projects and Amounts Released to NGOs, 1991-98

Period	Number of projects		US$ Amounts approved		US$ Amounts released	
	New	Cumulative	New	Cumulative	New	Cumulative
1990-91	464	472	158.54	158.91	106.60	112.03
1991-92	549	1,021	287.11	446.02	121.64	233.67
1992-93	626	1,647	399.88	845.91	195.71	429.38
1993-94	581	2,228	315.02	1160.93	171.01	600.38
1994-95	579	2,807	440.69	1601.62	209.50	809.89
1995-96	702	3,509	366.81	1968.43	259.30	1069.19
1996-97	746	4,255	246.50	2138.31	250.14	1277.72
1997-98 (through Nov. 97)	324	4,579	72.31	2083.53	84.79	1288.57

Note: Bureau was set up in 1990 so earlier data not available. Cumulative figures show data for existing projects, plus new projects, and less completed projects.
Source: NGO Affairs Bureau.

BIBLIOGRAPHY

Background papers

1. **Ravallion, M. and Q. Wodon**. 1997a. "Poor Areas, or Only Poor People?" Policy Research Working Paper 1798, World Bank, Washington, D.C. (*revised version, June 17, 1998*).

2. _____1997b. "Banking on the Poor? Branch Placement and Nonfarm Rural Development in Bangladesh." Policy Research Working Paper 1858, World Bank, Washington, D.C. (*revised version, June 22, 1997*).

3. _____1997c. "Evaluating a Targeted Social Program When Placement is Decentralized." Policy Research Paper, World Bank, Washington, D.C.

4. **Wodon, Q.** 1997a. "A Profile of Poverty in Bangladesh: 1983-1992," South Asia Regional Working Paper Series No. IDP-169, World Bank, Washington, D.C.

5. _____1997b. "Poverty in Bangladesh: Extent and Evolution." *Bangladesh Development Studies* 23 (3-4): 81-110.

6. _____1997c "Food Energy Intake and Cost of Basic Needs: Measuring Poverty in Bangladesh." *Journal of Development Studies* 34: 66-101.

7. _____1997d. "Targeting the Poor Using ROC Curves." *World Development*. 25 (12): 2083-92.

8. _____1998a. "Between Group Inequality and Targeted Transfers." Forthcoming in *Review of Income and Wealth*.

9. _____1998b. "Growth, Inequality and Poverty: A Regional Panel Model for Bangladesh." World Bank, Washington, D.C.

10. _____1998c. "Cost-Effectiveness of Food for Education in Bangladesh." World Bank, Washington, D.C.

11. _____1998d. "Micro Determinants of Consumption, Poverty, Growth, and Inequality in Bangladesh." World Bank, Washington, D.C.

Other references

Ahmed, A. U., and K. Billah. 1994. "Food for Education in Bangladesh: An Early Assessment." International Food Policy Research Institute, Washington, D.C, and Dhaka.

Ahmed, A. U., H. A. Khan, and R. K. Sampath. 1991. "Poverty in Bangladesh: Measurement, Decomposition, and Intertemporal Comparison." *Journal of Development Studies* 27: 48-63.

Ahuja, V., B. Bidani, F. Ferreira, and M. Walton. 1997. *Everyone's Miracle? Revisiting Poverty and Inequality in East Asia*. World Bank , Washington, D.C.

Asian Development Bank. 1992. *An Assessment of the Role of NGOs in Bangladesh*. Melbourne.

Association for Social Advancement. 1997. *Hard-core Poor in Microcredit*. Dhaka.

Bangladesh Bureau of Statistics. 1994a. *Child Nutrition Survey of Bangladesh 1992*. Dhaka.

_____1994b. *Report on the Survey on FFW - 1991*. Dhaka.

_____1994c. *Report on the Survey on Test Relief 1991*. Dhaka.

_____1994d. *Report on the Survey on Vulnerable Group Development 1991*. Dhaka.

_____1995. *Report of Household Expenditure Survey 1991-92*. Dhaka.

_____1996a. *Report of the Poverty Monitoring Survey 1995*. Dhaka.

_____1996b. *Report on Labour Force Survey in Bangladesh 1995-96*. Dhaka.

_____1997a. *Analysis of Basic Needs Dimension of Poverty, Volume II*. Dhaka.

_____1997b. *Child Nutrition Survey of Bangladesh 1995-96*. Dhaka.

_____997c. *Report on the Household Expenditure Survey 1991-92*. Dhaka

_____1997d. *Urban Poverty Monitoring Survey December 1995*. Dhaka.

_____1997e. *Summary Report of the Household Expenditure Survey 1995-96*. Dhaka.

_____1997f. *Basic Information on the Household Expenditure Survey 1995-96*. Dhaka.

Bangladesh Institute of Development Studies. 1997. "An Evaluation of the Food for Education Program: Enhancing Accessibility to and Retention in Primary Education for the Rural Poor in Bangladesh." Dhaka.

Bruno, M., M. Ravallion, and L. Squire. 1996. "Equity and Growth in Developing Countries." Policy Research Working Paper 1563. World Bank, Washington, D.C.

Chowdhury, N. 1992. "A Reassessment of Bangladesh's Poverty Record, 1974-1984." *Bangladesh Development Studies* 20(1): 1-24.

_____1993. "Reassessment of Poverty Record: A Further Comment on Osmani." *Bangladesh Development Studies* 21: 79-97.

CIRDAP (Center for Integrated Rural Development for Asia and the Pacific), 1997a, "Distribution of Benefits of Rural Public Expenditure on Education." Monitoring Adjustment and Poverty Policy Brief 7, Dhaka.

_____1997b. "Distributional Patterns of Public Health Spending in Rural Bangladesh". Monitoring Adjustment and Poverty Policy Brief 8, Dhaka.

_____1997c. "Structural Adjustment Policies and Labor Markets." Monitoring Adjustment and Poverty Policy Brief 11, Dhaka.

Cleland, J., J. F. Phillips, S. Amin, and G. M. Kamal. 1994. *The Determinants of Reproductive Change in Bangladesh: Success in a Challenging Environment.* Washington, D.C.: World Bank.

Datt, G., and M. Ravallion. 1992. "Growth and Redistribution Components of Changes in Poverty Measures: A Decomposition with Applications to Brazil and India in the 1980's" *Journal of Development Economics* 38: 275-295.

Deininger, K., and L. Squire. 1996. "New Ways of Looking at Old Issues: Inequality and Growth." World Bank, Washington, D.C.

del Ninno, C., and P. Dorosh. 1998. "Government Policy, Markets and Food Security in Bangladesh." IFPRI, Dhaka.

Dorosh, P., and S. Haggblade. 1995. "Filling the Gaps: Consolidating Evidence on the Design of Alternative Targeted Food Programmes in Bangladesh." *Bangladesh Development Studies* 23, No. 3&4: 47-80.

Easterly, W. 1989. "A Consistency Framework for Macroeconomic Analysis." Policy, Planning, and Research Working Paper 234, World Bank, Washington, D.C.

Fauveau V., A. Briend, J. Chakraborty, and A. B. Sarder. 1990. "The Contribution of Severe Malnutrition to Child Mortality in Rural Bangladesh: Implications for Targeting Nutritional Interventions. *Food and Nutrition Bulletin* 12: 215-19.

Filmer, D., E. M. King, and L. Pritchett. 1998. "Gender Disparity in South Asia." Policy Research Working paper 1867, World Bank, Washington, D.C.

Filmer, D., J. Hammer, and L. Pritchett. 1998. "Health Policy in Poor Countries: Weak Links in the Chain." Policy Research Working Paper 1874, World Bank, Washington, D.C.

Filmer, D., and L. Pritchett. 1997. "Child Mortality and Public Spending on Health: How Much Does Money Matter?" Policy Research Working Paper 1864, World Bank, Washington, D.C.

Foster, J., J. Greer, and E. Thorbecke. 1984. "A Class of Decomposable Poverty Measures." *Econometrica* 52: 761-66.

Government of Bangladesh, Ministry of Health and Family Welfare. 1997. "Health and Population Sector Strategy." Dhaka.

Government of Bangladesh, Planning Commission. 1997. "The Fifth Five Year Plan 1997-2002." Draft. Dhaka.

Greaney V., S. R. Khandker, and M. Alam. 1997. "Bangladesh: Assessing Basic Learning Skills." World Bank, Washington, D.C.

Haider, S. J., M. S. Hossain, Q. A. Samad, A. K. M. Islam, and M. Ahmed. 1997. "Case Specific Health Care Services Utilization and Health care Expenditures at Individual and Household Levels: Regional and Socio-Demographic Differentials 1994 and 1995." Bangladesh Bureau of Statistics, Dhaka.

Hossain, Z. R., and M. Hossain. (eds.) 1995. *Rethinking Rural Poverty: Bangladesh as a Case Study.* New York: Sage Publications.

Hossain, M., and B. Sen. 1992. "Rural Poverty in Bangladesh: Trends and Determinants." *Asian Development Review* 10(1): 1-34.

Khan, A. R. 1990. "Poverty in Bangladesh: A Consequence of and a Constraint on Growth." *Bangladesh Development Studies* 18(1): 19-34.

Khan, S. M., P. Montiel, and N. U. Haque. 1990. "Adjustment with Growth: Relating the Analytical Approaches of the IMF and the World Bank." *Journal of Development Studies* 32: 155-79.

Khandker, S. R. 1996. "Education Achievements and School Efficiency in Rural Bangladesh." World Bank Discussion Paper 319, Washington, D.C.

Khandker, S. R., and O. H. Chowdhury. 1996. "Targeted Credit Programs and Rural Poverty in Bangladesh." World Bank Discussion Paper 336, Washington, D.C.

Khandker S. R., B. Khalily, and Z. Khan. 1995. "Grameen Bank: Performance and Sustainability." World Bank Discussion Paper 306, Washington, D.C.

Khandker, S. R., Z. Khan, and B. Khalily. 1995. "Sustainability of a Government Targeted Credit Program: Evidence from Bangladesh." World Bank Discussion Paper 316, Washington, D.C.

Khundker, N., W. Mahmud, B. Sen, and M. U. Ahmad. 1994. "Urban Poverty in Bangladesh: Trends, Determinants, and Policy Issues." *Asian Development Review* 12(1): 1-31.

Kuznets, S. 1955. "Economic Growth and Income Inequality." *American Economic Review* 45(1): 1-28.

_____1963. "Quantitative Aspects of Economic Growth of Nations: VIII. Distribution of Income by Size." *Economic Development and Cultural Change* 12(1): 1-80.

Mabud M. A., M. S. Hossain, and A. Haque. 1997. "Socio-Economic Differentials of Some Reproductive Health Elements in Rural Bangladesh." Bangladesh Bureau of Statistics, Dhaka.

Mitchell, D. 1998. "Promoting Growth in Bangladesh Agriculture." World Bank, Washington D.C.

Murdoch, J. 1997. "The Microfinance Revolution." Department of Economics, Harvard University, Cambridge, Mass.

Oshima, H. T. 1962. "The International Comparison of Size Distribution of Family Income with Special Reference to Asia." *Review of Economics and Statistics* 54: 439-445.

Osmani, S. 1990. "Structural Change and Poverty in Bangladesh: The Case of a False Turning Point." *Bangladesh Development Studies* 18(1): 55-74.

Pitt and Khandker. 1998. "The Impact of Group-Based Credit Programs on Poor Households in Bangladesh: Does the Gender of Participants Matter?" Forthcoming in *Journal of Political Economy*

Psacharopoulos, G. 1994. "Returns to Investment in Education: A Global Update." *World Development* 22: 1325-43.

Rabbani G., M. S. Hossain, and T. Islam. 1997. "Health Care Expenditures in Bangladesh." Bangladesh Bureau of Statistics, Dhaka.

Rahman, R. I. 1996. "Impact of Credit for Rural Poor: An Evaluation of Palli Karma Sahayak Foundation's Credit Programme." Research Report 143, Bangladesh Institute for Development Studies, Dhaka.

Rahman, A., and T. Haque. 1988. "Poverty and Inequality in Bangladesh in the Eighties: An Analysis of Some Recent Evidence." Research Report 91, Bangladesh Institute for Development Studies, Dhaka.

Rahman, H.Z., M. Hossain (eds.), 1995. *Rethinking Rural Poverty: Bangladesh as a Case Study*. New York: Sage Publications.

Rahman, H. Z., M. Hossain, and B. Sen. 1996. *1987-1994: Dynamics of Rural Poverty in Bangladesh,* Dhaka: Bangladesh Institute for Development Studies.

Ravallion, M. 1990. "The Challenging Arithmetic of Poverty in Bangladesh." *Bangladesh Development Studies* 18: 75-87.

_____1994. *Poverty Comparisons*. Chur, Switzerland: Harwood Academic Press

_____1995. "Household Vulnerability to Aggregate Shocks: Differing Fortunes for the Poor in Bangladesh and Indonesia." In K. Basu, P. Patanaik, and K. Suzumara, eds*., Choice Welfare and Development*. Oxford: Clarendon Press.

_____1997. "Can High Inequality Developing Countries Escape Absolute Poverty?" *Economics Letters* 56: 51-57.

Ravallion, M., and B. Bidani. 1994. "How Robust is a Poverty Profile*?" World Bank Economic Review* 8: 75-102.

Ravallion, M., and M. Huppi. 1991. "Measuring Changes in Poverty: A Methodological Case Study of Indonesia During an Adjustment Period." *World Bank Economic Review* 5: 57-84.

Ravallion, M., and B. Sen. 1994. "Impacts on Rural Poverty of Land-Based Targeting: Further Results for Bangladesh." *World Development*, 22(6): 823-38.

_____1996. "When Method Matters: Toward Resolution of the Debate about Bangladesh's Poverty Measures." *Economic Development and Cultural Change* 44: 761-792.

Ray, D. 1998. *Development Economics*. Princeton: Princeton University Press.

Sen, A.K. 1984. *Resources, Values and Development*. Cambridge, Mass: Harvard University Press.

Sen, B. 1995. "Rural Poverty Trends: 1963-64 to 1983-90." In Z. R. Hossain and M. Hossain, eds., *Rethinking Rural Poverty: Bangladesh as a Case Study*. New York: Sage Publications.

Sen, B., and Q. T. Islam. 1993. "Monitoring Adjustment and Urban Poverty in Bangladesh: Issues, Dimensions, Tendencies." In *Monitoring Adjustment and Poverty in Bangladesh, Report on the Framework Project*, CIRDAP Study Series 160. Dhaka: Center for Integrated Rural Development for Asia and the Pacific.

Subbarao, K., A. Bonnerjee, J. Braithwaite, S. Carvalho, K. Ezemenari, C. Graham, and A. Thompson. 1997. *Safety Net Programs and Poverty Reduction: Lessons from Cross-country Experience*, Washington, D.C.: World Bank.

Summers, L. H. 1994. "Investing in All the People, Economic Development Institute." EDI Seminar Paper 45, World Bank, Washington, D.C.

UNICEF.1998. *State of the World's Children*, Oxford: Oxford University Press.

World Bank. 1990. *Bangladesh - Poverty and Public Expenditures: An Evaluation of the Impact of Selected Government Programs*. Washington, D.C.

_____1996a. *Bangladesh Education Expenditure Review*. Washington, D.C.

_____1996b. *Bangladesh: Rural Infrastructure Strategy Study*. Washington, D.C.

_____1996c. *Pursuing Common Goals: Strengthening Relations between Government and Development NGOs*. Washington, D.C.

_____1996d. *Bangladesh: Public Expenditure Review*. Washington, D.C.

_____1997a. *Bangladesh: Annual Economic Update 1997*. Washington, D.C.

_____1997b. *Bangladesh: The Non-Farm Sector in a Diversifying Rural Economy*. Washington, D.C.

_____1997c. *Making the Best Use of Public Resources: Bangladesh Public Expenditure Review 1997 Update*. Washington, D.C.

_____1997d. *Municipal Finance Management Sector Study*. 1997, *Washington, D.C.*

Distributors of World Bank Group Publications

Prices and credit terms vary from country to country. Consult your local distributor before placing an order.

ARGENTINA
World Publications SA
Av. Cordoba 1877
1120 Ciudad de Buenos Aires
Tel: (54 11) 4815-8156
Fax: (54 11) 4815-8156
E-mail: wpbooks@infovia.com.ar

AUSTRALIA, FIJI, PAPUA NEW GUINEA, SOLOMON ISLANDS, VANUATU, AND SAMOA
D.A. Information Services
648 Whitehorse Road
Mitcham 3132, Victoria
Tel: (61) 3 9210 7777
Fax: (61) 3 9210 7788
E-mail: service@dadirect.com.au
URL: http://www.dadirect.com.au

AUSTRIA
Gerold and Co.
Weihburggasse 26
A-1011 Wien
Tel: (43 1) 512-47-31-0
Fax: (43 1) 512-47-31-29
URL: http://www.gerold.co/at.online

BANGLADESH
Micro Industries Development
Assistance Society (MIDAS)
House 5, Road 16
Dhanmondi R/Area
Dhaka 1209
Tel: (880 2) 326427
Fax: (880 2) 811188

BELGIUM
Jean De Lannoy
Av. du Roi 202
1060 Brussels
Tel: (32 2) 538-5169
Fax: (32 2) 538-0841

BRAZIL
Publicacões Tecnicas Internacionais Ltda.
Rua Peixoto Gomide, 209
01409 Sao Paulo, SP.
Tel: (55 11) 259-6644
Fax: (55 11) 258-6990
E-mail: postmaster@pti.uol.br
URL: http://www.uol.br

CANADA
Renouf Publishing Co. Ltd.
5369 Canotek Road
Ottawa, Ontario K1J 9J3
Tel: (613) 745-2665
Fax: (613) 745-7660
E-mail:
  order.dept@renoufbooks.com
URL: http:// www.renoufbooks.com

CHINA
China Financial & Economic
Publishing House
8, Da Fo Si Dong Jie
Beijing
Tel: (86 10) 6401-7365
Fax: (86 10) 6401-7365

China Book Import Centre
P.O. Box 2825
Beijing

Chinese Corporation for Promotion
of Humanities
52, You Fang Hu Tong,
Xuan Nei Da Jie
Beijing
Tel: (86 10) 660 72 494
Fax: (86 10) 660 72 494

COLOMBIA
Infoenlace Ltda.
Carrera 6 No. 51-21
Apartado Aereo 34270
Santafé de Bogotá, D.C.
Tel: (57 1) 285-2798
Fax: (57 1) 285-2798

COTE D'IVOIRE
Center d'Edition et de Diffusion
Africaines (CEDA)
04 B.P. 541
Abidjan 04
Tel: (225) 24 6510; 24 6511
Fax: (225) 25 0567

CYPRUS
Center for Applied Research
Cyprus College
6, Diogenes Street, Engomi
P.O. Box 2006
Nicosia
Tel: (357 2) 59-0730
Fax: (357 2) 66-2051

CZECH REPUBLIC
USIS, NIS Prodejna
Havelkova 22
130 00 Prague 3
Tel: (420 2) 2423 1486
Fax: (420 2) 2423 1114
URL: http://www.nis.cz/

DENMARK
SamfundsLitteratur
Rosenoerns Allé 11
DK-1970 Frederiksberg C
Tel: (45 35) 351942
Fax: (45 35) 357822
URL: http://www.sl.cbs.dk

ECUADOR
Libri Mundi
Libreria Internacional
P.O. Box 17-01-3029
Juan Leon Mera 851
Quito
Tel: (593 2) 521-606; (593 2) 544-185
Fax: (593 2) 504-209
E-mail: librimu1@librimundi.com.ec
E-mail: librimu2@librimundi.com.ec

CODEU
Ruiz de Castilla 763, Edif. Expocolor
Primer piso, Of. #2
Quito
Tel/Fax: (593 2) 507-383; 253-091
E-mail: codeu@impsat.net.ec

EGYPT, ARAB REPUBLIC OF
Al Ahram Distribution Agency
Al Galaa Street
Cairo
Tel: (20 2) 578-6083
Fax: (20 2) 578-6833

The Middle East Observer
41, Sherif Street
Cairo
Tel: (20 2) 393-9732
Fax: (20 2) 393-9732

FINLAND
Akateeminen Kirjakauppa
P.O. Box 128
FIN-00101 Helsinki
Tel: (358 0) 121 4418
Fax: (358 0) 121-4435
E-mail: akatilaus@stockmann.fi
URL: http://www.akateeminen.com

FRANCE
Editions Eska; DBJ
48, rue Gay Lussac
75005 Paris
Tel: (33-1) 55-42-73-08
Fax: (33-1) 43-29-91-67

GERMANY
UNO-Verlag
Poppelsdorfer Allee 55
53115 Bonn
Tel: (49 228) 949020
Fax: (49 228) 217492
URL: http://www.uno-verlag.de
E-mail: unoverlag@aol.com

GHANA
Epp Books Services
P.O. Box 44
TUC
Accra
Tel: 223 21 778843
Fax: 223 21 779099

GREECE
Papasotiriou S.A.
35, Stournara Str.
106 82 Athens
Tel: (30 1) 364-1826
Fax: (30 1) 364-8254

HAITI
Culture Diffusion
5, Rue Capois
C.P. 257
Port-au-Prince
Tel: (509) 23 9260
Fax: (509) 23 4858

HONG KONG, CHINA; MACAO
Asia 2000 Ltd.
Sales & Circulation Department
302 Seabird House
22-28 Wyndham Street, Central
Hong Kong, China
Tel: (852) 2530-1409
Fax: (852) 2526-1107
E-mail: sales@asia2000.com.hk
URL: http://www.asia2000.com.hk

HUNGARY
Euro Info Service
Margitszgeti Europa Haz
H-1138 Budapest
Tel: (36 1) 350 80 24, 350 80 25
Fax: (36 1) 350 90 32
E-mail: euroinfo@mail.matav.hu

INDIA
Allied Publishers Ltd.
751 Mount Road
Madras - 600 002
Tel: (91 44) 852-3938
Fax: (91 44) 852-0649

INDONESIA
Pt. Indira Limited
Jalan Borobudur 20
P.O. Box 181
Jakarta 10320
Tel: (62 21) 390-4290
Fax: (62 21) 390-4289

IRAN
Ketab Sara Co. Publishers
Khaled Eslamboli Ave., 6th Street
Delafrooz Alley No. 8
P.O. Box 15745-733
Tehran 15117
Tel: (98 21) 8717819; 8716104
Fax: (98 21) 8712479
E-mail: ketab-sara@neda.net.ir

Kowkab Publishers
P.O. Box 19575-511
Tehran
Tel: (98 21) 258-3723
Fax: (98 21) 258-3723

IRELAND
Government Supplies Agency
Oifig an tSoláthair
4-5 Harcourt Road
Dublin 2
Tel: (353 1) 661-3111
Fax: (353 1) 475-2670

ISRAEL
Yozmot Literature Ltd.
P.O. Box 56055
3 Yohanan Hasandlar Street
Tel Aviv 61560
Tel: (972 3) 5285-397
Fax: (972 3) 5285-397

R.O.Y. International
PO Box 13056
Tel Aviv 61130
Tel: (972 3) 649 9469
Fax: (972 3) 648 6039
E-mail: royil@netvision.net.il
URL: http://www.royint.co.il

Palestinian Authority/Middle East
Index Information Services
P.O.B. 19502 Jerusalem
Tel: (972 2) 6271219
Fax: (972 2) 6271634

ITALY, LIBERIA
Licosa Commissionaria Sansoni SPA
Via Duca Di Calabria, 1/1
Casella Postale 552
50125 Firenze
Tel: (39 55) 645-415
Fax: (39 55) 641-257
E-mail: licosa@ftbcc.it
URL: http://www.ftbcc.it/licosa

JAMAICA
Ian Randle Publishers Ltd.
206 Old Hope Road, Kingston 6
Tel: 876-927-2085
Fax: 876-977-0243
E-mail: irpl@colis.com

JAPAN
Eastern Book Service
3-13 Hongo 3-chome, Bunkyo-ku
Tokyo 113
Tel: (81 3) 3818-0861
Fax: (81 3) 3818-0864
E-mail: orders@svt-ebs.co.jp
URL:
  http://www.bekkoame.or.jp/~svt-ebs

KENYA
Africa Book Service (E.A.) Ltd.
Quaran House, Mfangano Street
P.O. Box 45245
Nairobi
Tel: (254 2) 223 641
Fax: (254 2) 330 272

Legacy Books
Loita House
Mezzanine 1
P.O. Box 68077
Nairobi
Tel: (254) 2-330853, 221426
Fax: (254) 2-330854, 561654
E-mail: Legacy@form-net.com

KOREA, REPUBLIC OF
Dayang Books Trading Co.
International Division
783-20, Pangba Bon-Dong,
Socho-ku
Seoul
Tel: (82 2) 536-9555
Fax: (82 2) 536-0025
E-mail: seamap@chollian.net

Eulyoo Publishing Co., Ltd.
46-1, Susong-Dong
Jongro-Gu
Seoul
Tel: (82 2) 734-3515
Fax: (82 2) 732-9154

LEBANON
Librairie du Liban
P.O. Box 11-9232
Beirut
Tel: (961 9) 217 944
Fax: (961 9) 217 434
E-mail: hsayegh@librairie-du-liban.com.lb
URL: http://www.librairie-du-liban.com.lb

MALAYSIA
University of Malaya Cooperative
Bookshop, Limited
P.O. Box 1127
Jalan Pantai Baru
59700 Kuala Lumpur
Tel: (60 3) 756-5000
Fax: (60 3) 755-4424
E-mail: umkoop@tm.net.my

MEXICO
INFOTEC
Av. San Fernando No. 37
Col. Toriello Guerra
14050 Mexico, D.F.
Tel: (52 5) 624-2800
Fax: (52 5) 624-2822
E-mail: infotec@rtn.net.mx
URL: http://rtn.net.mx

Mundi-Prensa Mexico S.A. de C.V.
c/Rio Panuco, 141-Colonia
Cuauhtemoc
06500 Mexico, D.F.
Tel: (52 5) 533-5658
Fax: (52 5) 514-6799

NEPAL
Everest Media International Services
(P.) Ltd.
GPO Box 5443
Kathmandu
Tel: (977 1) 416 026
Fax: (977 1) 224 431

NETHERLANDS
De Lindeboom/Internationale
Publicaties b.v.-
P.O. Box 202, 7480 AE Haaksbergen
Tel: (31 53) 574-0004
Fax: (31 53) 572-9296
E-mail: lindeboo@worldonline.nl
URL: http://www.worldonline.nl/-lindeboo

NEW ZEALAND
EBSCO NZ Ltd.
Private Mail Bag 99914
New Market
Auckland
Tel: (64 9) 524-8119
Fax: (64 9) 524-8067

Oasis Official
P.O. Box 3627
Wellington
Tel: (64 4) 499 1551
Fax: (64 4) 499 1972
E-mail: oasis@actrix.gen.nz
URL: http://www.oasisbooks.co.nz/

NIGERIA
University Press Limited
Three Crowns Building Jericho
Private Mail Bag 5095
Ibadan
Tel: (234 22) 41-1356
Fax: (234 22) 41-2056

PAKISTAN
Mirza Book Agency
65, Shahrah-e-Quaid-e-Azam
Lahore 54000
Tel: (92 42) 735 3601
Fax: (92 42) 576 3714

Oxford University Press
5 Bangalore Town
Sharae Faisal
PO Box 13033
Karachi-75350
Tel: (92 21) 446307
Fax: (92 21) 4547640
E-mail: ouppak@TheOffice.net

Pak Book Corporation
Aziz Chambers 21, Queen's Road
Lahore
Tel: (92 42) 636 3222; 636 0885
Fax: (92 42) 636 2328
E-mail: pbc@brain.net.pk

PERU
Editorial Desarrollo SA
Apartado 3824, Ica 242 OF. 106
Lima 1
Tel: (51 14) 285380
Fax: (51 14) 286628

PHILIPPINES
International Booksource Center Inc.
1127-A Antipolo St, Barangay,
Venezuela
Makati City
Tel: (63 2) 896 6501; 6505; 6507
Fax: (63 2) 896 1741

POLAND
International Publishing Service
Ul. Piekna 31/37
00-677 Warzawa
Tel: (48 2) 628-6089
Fax: (48 2) 621-7255
E-mail: books%ips@ikp.atm.com.pl
URL:
  http://www.ipscg.waw.pl/ips/export

PORTUGAL
Livraria Portugal
Apartado 2681, Rua Do Carm
o 70-74
1200 Lisbon
Tel: (1) 347-4982
Fax: (1) 347-0264

ROMANIA
Compani De Librarii Bucuresti S.A.
Str. Lipscani no. 26, sector 3
Bucharest
Tel: (40 1) 313 9645
Fax: (40 1) 312 4000

RUSSIAN FEDERATION
Isdatelstvo <Ves Mir>
9a, Kolpachniy Pereulok
Moscow 101831
Tel: (7 095) 917 87 49
Fax: (7 095) 917 92 59
ozimarin@glasnet.ru

**SINGAPORE; TAIWAN, CHINA
MYANMAR; BRUNEI**
Hemisphere Publication Services
41 Kallang Pudding Road #04-03
Golden Wheel Building
Singapore 349316
Tel: (65) 741-5166
Fax: (65) 742-9356
E-mail: ashgate@asianconnect.com

SLOVENIA
Gospodarski vestnik Publishing
Group
Dunajska cesta 5
1000 Ljubljana
Tel: (386 61) 133 83 47; 132 12 30
Fax: (386 61) 133 80 30
E-mail: repansekj@gvestnik.si

SOUTH AFRICA, BOTSWANA
For single titles:
Oxford University Press Southern
Africa
Vasco Boulevard, Goodwood
P.O. Box 12119, N1 City 7463
Cape Town
Tel: (27 21) 595 4400
Fax: (27 21) 595 4430
E-mail: oxford@oup.co.za

For subscription orders:
International Subscription Service
P.O. Box 41095
Craighall
Johannesburg 2024
Tel: (27 11) 880-1448
Fax: (27 11) 880-6248
E-mail: iss@is.co.za

SPAIN
Mundi-Prensa Libros, S.A.
Castello 37
28001 Madrid
Tel: (34 91) 4 363700
Fax: (34 91) 5 753998
E-mail: libreria@mundiprensa.es
URL: http://www.mundiprensa.com/

Mundi-Prensa Barcelona
Consell de Cent, 391
08009 Barcelona
Tel: (34 3) 488-3492
Fax: (34 3) 487-7659
E-mail: barcelona@mundiprensa.es

SRI LANKA, THE MALDIVES
Lake House Bookshop
100, Sir Chittampalam Gardiner
Mawatha
Colombo 2
Tel: (94 1) 32105
Fax: (94 1) 432104
E-mail: LHL@sri.lanka.net

SWEDEN
Wennergren-Williams AB
P. O. Box 1305
S-171 25 Solna
Tel: (46 8) 705-97-50
Fax: (46 8) 27-00-71
E-mail: mail@wwi.se

SWITZERLAND
Librairie Payot Service Institutionnel
C(tm)tes-de-Montbenon 30
1002 Lausanne
Tel: (41 21) 341-3229
Fax: (41 21) 341-3235

ADECO Van Diermen
EditionsTechniques
Ch. de Lacuez 41
CH1807 Blonay
Tel: (41 21) 943 2673
Fax: (41 21) 943 3605

THAILAND
Central Books Distribution
306 Silom Road
Bangkok 10500
Tel: (66 2) 2336930-9
Fax: (66 2) 237-8321

**TRINIDAD & TOBAGO
AND THE CARRIBBEAN**
Systematics Studies Ltd.
St. Augustine Shopping Center
Eastern Main Road, St. Augustine
Trinidad & Tobago, West Indies
Tel: (868) 645-8466
Fax: (868) 645-8467
E-mail: tobe@trinidad.net

UGANDA
Gustro Ltd.
PO Box 9997, Madhvani Building
Plot 16/4 Jinja Rd.
Kampala
Tel: (256 41) 251 467
Fax: (256 41) 251 468
E-mail: gus@swiftuganda.com

UNITED KINGDOM
Microinfo Ltd.
P.O. Box 3, Omega Park, Alton,
Hampshire GU34 2PG
England
Tel: (44 1420) 86848
Fax: (44 1420) 89889
E-mail: wbank@microinfo.co.uk
URL: http://www.microinfo.co.uk

The Stationery Office
51 Nine Elms Lane
London SW8 5DR
Tel: (44 171) 873-8400
Fax: (44 171) 873-8242
URL: http://www.the-stationery-office.co.uk/

VENEZUELA
Tecni-Ciencia Libros, S.A.
Centro Cuidad Comercial Tamanco
Nivel C2, Caracas
Tel: (58 2) 959 5547; 5035; 0016
Fax: (58 2) 959 5636

ZAMBIA
University Bookshop, University of
Zambia
Great East Road Campus
P.O. Box 32379
Lusaka
Tel: (260 1) 252 576
Fax: (260 1) 253 952

ZIMBABWE
Academic and Baobab Books (Pvt.)
Ltd.
4 Conald Road, Graniteside
P.O. Box 567
Harare
Tel: 263 4 755035
Fax: 263 4 781913